D0758160

EQUAL *to the* CHALLENGE

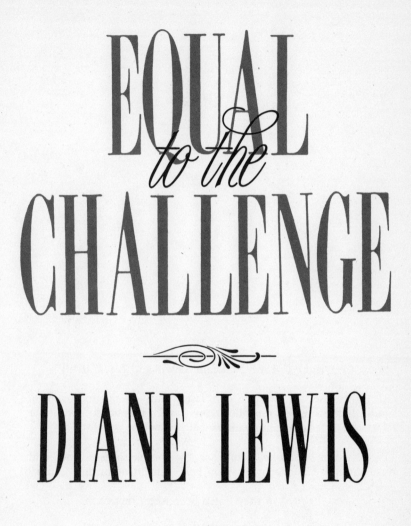

EQUAL
to the
CHALLENGE

DIANE LEWIS

THOMAS NELSON PUBLISHERS
Nashville

Copyright © 1988 by Diane Lewis and J. J. Carroll

All rights reserved. Written permission must be secured from the publishers to use or reproduce any part of this book, except for brief quotations in critical reviews or articles.

Published in Nashville, Tennessee, by Thomas Nelson, Inc., and distributed in Canada by Lawson Falle, Ltd., Cambridge, Ontario.

Printed in the United States of America.

Library of Congress Cataloging-in-Publication Data

Lewis, Diane, 1936-
  Why women fail in business.

  1. Sex role in the work environment. 2. Women—
Psychology. 3. Women in business. 4. Success in
business. 5. Promotions. I. Carroll, Joe. II. Title.
HD6054.3.L48 1987   658.4'09088042   87-15370
ISBN 0-8407-4219-3

1 2 3 4 5 6 7—92 91 90 89 88

To Carroll Ritzke,
my partner
and friend

Acknowledgments

To Jill Muck,
my publicist,
I give my continued thanks
and appreciation.

CONTENTS

Introduction

"A woman shouldn't try to act like a man."

I heard that remark somewhere in the answer of every woman I interviewed for this book when I asked, "What do you think about women in business?" Every one. It was a universal reaction.

Of course, I've said the same thing myself; we all have. But I found that gathering material for a book is different from simple conversation. It makes one examine everything much more closely. For the first time, I found myself wondering exactly what we all mean when we talk about acting "like a man" or "like a woman," particularly when we're talking about business and about working. Is there something about the job behavior of us women that sets us apart?

Eventually, I focused on a stereotype about women that I'd never consciously examined before. I decided that the stereotype was valid. It was a reluctant admission that had unpleasant overtones.

We women *are* different.

Not just in the physical sense; that's obvious. But in dozens of more subtle ways; in our attitudes, our values, and our temperaments. Those internal differences lead to one very big external difference. We women often behave in ways contrary to our success, even to our survival, in the world of work.

I didn't fully realize this until I was reading an article in a popular business magazine recently. The article demanded to know why there weren't more stories in the magazine about prominent businesswomen. The writer concluded that the reason was that there weren't very many of us. The article got me to thinking seriously about why we women are not as successful in the working world as I feel we should be.

Not that we're failures—far from it. It's easy to find stories and biographical material on women in the media, in entertainment, in sports. But when it comes to business, I get the feeling that we can do better. This is particularly the case in the higher level management ranks and even more so among entrepreneurs, those of us who start our own businesses.

It's too easy to answer that the right of women to hold positions of power has been recognized so recently that we haven't yet had a chance to develop into those positions. It's too easy to say that we'll do better as time goes on.

It's unreasonable to continue waiting for our success. More should have happened by now. *The Feminine Mystique* was published nearly a quarter century ago, which puts us into the second generation of the women's movement. We women should be planning comfortable retirements by this time after successful careers. Instead, most of us are still trying to make it. Wouldn't you expect a child of yours to have "found herself" by the time she was more than twenty years out of school? Can we women excuse ourselves from the standards we set for our own children? How come we haven't "found ourselves" yet? How come we haven't "hit our stride," "hit the ground running," or "hit a homer," as often as we should have by now? How long does it take to build a career, anyway?

The reason for our unacceptably slow pace is one you might not like to hear. It's one that will require you to accept as true some of the uncomplimentary stereotypes that I had to acknowledge.

I believe the reason is that we women often behave differently and—I'm embarrassed to have to say—inappropriately in the working world. Women in general have habits that cause them to commit the same errors in their working lives time after time after time. And the more serious a woman is about her career, the more costly are those errors. Indeed, for the most professional among us, they're fatal.

Sociologist Emile Durkheim was the first to describe the condition of unrest and alienation that follows a breakdown of familiar values. People have a limited capacity for change which, when overwhelmed, results in what Alvin Toffler called future shock. Is it a surprise that we women who work suffer from the kind of difficulty that Durkheim and Toffler were trying to characterize? Is it a surprise that this dissociation manifests itself in counterproductive behavior? Shouldn't we have expected trouble from the first hint of the emergent female—confusion, adjustment problems, resentment? As Woodrow Wilson said, "If you want to make enemies, try to change something."

And look at the changes in *us*. We were born to a social contract in which each of us was to play the supportive role of wife, mother, and homemaker exclusively and forever. We emerged as women into an entirely different social order in which each of us is expected to be assertive, competitive, and successful. And we've been expected to make this about-face in a single generation.

We were programmed by our society's expectations to behave one way as girls, then programmed to behave exactly the opposite way as women. No one should be expected to keep up. The wonder isn't that so many of us are having problems in the workplace; the wonder is that so many of us are doing well in spite of the tremendous pressures applied to us. If we women have a mass identity crisis that shows up as inappropriate work behavior, it's because we were set up for it.

I became convinced of this from more than twenty years of experience with Interviewing Dynamics, the personnel consulting company I founded. The nature of the recruiting industry is such that the majority of the people we've seen on behalf of our client companies have been women. After all that time dealing with real people in a real world rather than cardboard people in a textbook, I found myself wanting to share my observations with you.

I *want* to share them with you, but I don't *need* to. My

personnel business became rather successful over time. A few years ago, I decided to use my newfound freedom to put to work all that I'd learned from observing other women through my personnel business. I decided to work in one of the few remaining occupations where I wasn't allowed: Middle Eastern trade. I knew that I'd do well there, because I didn't know of any other woman working in the capacity of a *wasta,* a go-between, for the Arab sheikhs.

I knew that would add to my value, because the scarcer something is, other things being equal, the more it costs. Being the only woman in that business, being a unique commodity, was certain to bring me a lot of money. Of course, I realized at the time that the sheikhs might not see it exactly that way. But I sincerely thought I was the one to alter cultural aversion to dealing with and through a woman. And let's be honest: constant travel all over the world can be a real kick. All I had to do was make it work.

My friends all insisted that being a woman was two strikes against me. Some of them also said that my Christian faith was the third strike. On the contrary, however, most Arabs are devout and respect religious fervor in others. It implies that one is likely to possess the qualities that all astute businesspeople, Arabs included, esteem in their associates: determination, reliability, and, most important, integrity.

As a private pilot and aircraft owner, I felt at least minimally qualified to broker airframes to the Arab countries, which is how I started in the part of the Gulf known as the Emirates. The company I started, International Consultants, continues to be a factor in the brokerage of air transport over there, although we have since become better known for activities as diverse as metals brokerage and aquaculture. But convincing the sheikhs initially to accept both my qualifications and my earnest was a real challenge. They just weren't prepared at first to treat me as anything more than an object of curiosity. A lot of time and travel went by before that changed.

All that travel taught me about the importance of culture on the development of personality, among other things. I came to see how easily we American women might have had different expectations and habits if our culture had been different. It helped me understand that some of the habits programmed into *me* as a modern American woman had to be changed if I was to be effective in a radically different culture.

Establishing my *bona fides* in the Middle East took time and work, and it also took a change in my behavior. But—and this is the important part—that behavior change did not require me to "act like a man." It required me to show courage, determination, self-confidence, and faith, which are all female traits, as I'll explain in this book. They're also traits that *you* possess in abundance and that you can employ to your benefit.

No, I don't need to sell books for a living, and I'm not trying to build a constituency for public office. Here's the only reason I'm writing this book: I'm tired of watching other women self-destruct.

I believe that we women are sometimes our own worst enemies, damaging our chances for success and happiness because we behave unconsciously in ways that draw attention away from all the good of which we're capable. I believe we sometimes obscure our own talent, letting others concentrate on how we act socially rather than on how we perform professionally. I believe that allows a biased boss an easy way out. It permits focusing on "personality" or "organizational fit" rather than on an individual's results.

The good news is that if you stop committing those fatal errors, you'll have a degree of success that corresponds more closely to your God-given abilities than to the whims of a management that you would be foolish to assume is always on your side.

I also believe that—no, I *insist* that we women are bright enough and brave enough to do anything we want to in the working world. We are equal to the challenge. That's why the level at which you work is not important to me. If you choose a supportive role in the working world, that's great. If you choose to be in charge of everybody who's in those supportive roles, that's great, too. No matter what you do, no matter where you work, no matter how high or how low you are on the corporate ladder, I want to talk to *you* if you're a woman who works, because we all hinder ourselves the same ways.

You're entitled to a word of warning, though, before you get too involved: this is not a "How-to-Get-Ahead" book. I can't tell you how to do all those things that getting ahead on your job requires. Go to school or see your supervisor for that kind of help. I wish I had been able in good conscience to make this one of those "How-to-Make-a-Million" books filled with glittering generalities. But there are plenty of those around, and you don't need another.

Instead of talking about what you should do to succeed, we'll concentrate on what you must *stop* doing that stands in your way on the road to success.

In a nutshell, then, you're not getting ahead fast enough because *you're making errors* of job behavior. And if you don't stop making those errors, you won't meet your success goals *no matter how limited those goals might be and no matter how much you want them.* Furthermore, you make these particular errors *because you are a woman.* And worst of all, *you probably don't even know you're making them.*

CHAPTER 1

Understanding Our Early Programming

My father used to tell a story about the day I was born. The onset of my mother's labor had been so early and so sudden that it caught them both by surprise. The woman who lived upstairs accompanied my mother to the hospital and then called my father at work. She told him that there was no immediate need for him, that he might as well stay at work for the time being, and that she would call him when it was near time.

Of course, he couldn't keep his mind on the job. After a preoccupied half-hour or so, he asked his boss for the afternoon off. On his way to the hospital, he stopped to get some presents to commemorate the joyous occasion to come. For the guys at the plant, a box of cheap cigars. For my mother, of course, flowers and candy. And for me . . . a football.

I was already among those present when he got to the hospital. He used to tell how embarrassed he was to have brought a boy's toy for his child who turned out to be a daughter. He couldn't even view me in the nursery until he pulled a pink ribbon off some flowers and wrapped it as best he could around the football. Somehow, he felt, that made everything all right. Then he was able to unself-consciously wiggle the football at me through the nursery window. And that's how we met.

Dad's choice of a football made no difference to me, of course. A newborn can't tell a football from a teddy bear anyway. But it mattered to *him*. Like all of us, he felt an almost inescapable need to preserve one of our deepest identities, the social difference between male and female.

That's probably how we all acquired some of our first concepts about what it means to be "feminine," back there with good old pink and blue. Not much, is it? And yet such badges of distinction, effective in spite of their artificiality, can create over the course of a lifetime an environment that virtually controls the way a woman perceives herself. Recognizing, understanding, and dealing with the programming composed of those distinctions is critical for us to overcome the mistakes we women make in our working lives.

• *How We Came to Be "Programmed"* •

If you find yourself asking "What programming?" we're off to a good start. As children, we all received a great deal of informal training that defined for each of us what it means to be feminine. The distinction between pink and blue was only the beginning of training that was designed to mold us to the social model of "how little girls behave." It was both verbal and nonverbal, sometimes obvious and sometimes not.

Such training was always thorough and pervasive, however; so much so that most of us were no more aware of its influence on us than a fish is aware of the water in which it swims. As a result, our notion of femininity has been so ingrained in all of us that defining our early training further would be superfluous. All you need do to recover the specifics of your early programming is to think about it a bit. Can you remember your parents' challenging, "Can't you behave like a lady?" the disapproving looks you drew whenever you behaved assertively? your teacher's warning, "Little ladies don't act that way"? how they made you take subjects, play games, and admire heroes that were all different from what your brother was encouraged to take, play, and admire? how his future was

2

open to family discussion, while yours was already pre-destined? how he seemed freer than you because that's the way parents and teachers treated him?

The kind of intense and absolute indoctrination that we've been talking about might well be called conditioning or even brainwashing, but I prefer to call it *programming*. To me the word *programming* conveys an image of the way a computer is made to function: mindlessly, without any judgment for whether its tasks make sense.

The computer programmers have a saying: "Garbage in, garbage out." It emphasizes that the computer can only deal with the world in the ways its programs prepare it to, and as we all know, the programs aren't always perfect. It sometimes happens that some of the instructions necessary to the proper running of a program are inadvertently left out or incorrectly stated during the programming process. The computer seldom complains about the inadequacy of such a program; instead, it just produces wrong answers. The programmer then has to back up, analyze the program to find out what's missing, and change the program.

Many of us women suffer from a program that's faulty in terms of the challenges presented to us by the modern world. And, just like that computer, we can be unaware of the fault. That causes us to "produce the wrong answers" in terms of our careers. It's good that, unlike the computer, you and I can reprogram ourselves once we know there's a problem.

The object of our early programming was to produce women who would be wives, mothers, and homemakers. What made it work so well was that it was subtle and some-times even unconscious. Subtlety, of course, makes con-ditioning most effective, as shown by the story retold by all first-year psychology students about the two laboratory rats talking to one another. One of the rats says of their experi-menter, "Every time I press this lever, she gives me some food. I've really got her trained well, haven't I?"

Somebody is pressing *your* lever, and you may be no more aware of it than is that naive experimenter, so subtle has been your early programming. The object of this chapter is to make you conscious that you have been programmed beginning with the moment of your birth and continuing to the present time. Only with awareness of that fact will you see in the succeeding chapters the effects it has had on your behavior.

For example, are there certain jobs for which you've never even thought of applying, even though they pay lots more than you're making now? You'll read in chapter 2 how accepting jobs traditionally held by women holds us all back. And what's your excuse for not having applied for those higher-paying jobs? Because they're somehow not "ladylike"? Chapter 11 explains why fear of losing your femininity because of the kind of work you do is a fallacy. Or have you held back from those jobs because you feel you're "too good" for that kind of work? There's another chapter that tells how you're being programmed, even today, to have an ego that works against your success.

You see how it goes? The unconscious, unspoken, unrecognized attitudes programmed into you since childhood make you behave in ways that present barriers to your business success.

• We've All Been Programmed •

Besides being subtle, our programming is universal. We're all its victims. So I think we can discuss our early programming as though it were about the same for all of us while still acknowledging that our childhoods may have been very different. That is, even though when we were little girls we exhibited a wide range of behavior styles, from the precious porcelain doll to the grubby little tomboy, the essentials of our programming represent a common core of experience.

I was a complete tomboy, for example, and my memories are of playing baseball and even football far more than of playing house. As a consequence, my childhood programming gave me the experiences of teamwork, leadership, and determination that competitive sports provide. It's the kind of positive programming that's too often denied to our daughters, and it holds them back later in business life. As the Duke of Wellington said, "The Battle of Waterloo was won on the playing fields of Eton." To the extent that we deny our daughters access to these playing fields and the experience of winning (and losing), we deny them the chance to develop essential parts of their personalities. I'm glad I was spared that most-common technique of female programming: being told, when I came in dirty and bruised, "Little girls don't do things like that."

But even my early exposure to male-dominated activities did not preclude my having the same core experiences as the little girl down the block who wore only pinafores and who brought her dollies to watch the games in which I played. She was being programmed to tend toward being passive and quiet, traits usually associated with females; I was permitted to tend more toward being active and assertive, traits usually *not* associated with females. But these minor differences notwithstanding, we were both told about all the things that would happen "when you grow up and get married," "when you have your own home," and "when you have a family to take care of." That was really our *deep* programming.

Notice that I used the word *when*. I don't remember ever hearing the word *if* when talking about my supposed future as a homemaker, and I'll bet you don't either. It made me feel sometimes that there would be no options for me, that my horizons were limited to the role for which biology had suited me. Perhaps even worse, I don't remember anyone's ever asking me the question that was so commonly asked of my brother and the other boys in the neighborhood, "What do you want to be when you grow up?" They assumed that what I would automatically want to be was someone's wife and someone's mother and the maker of their home.

That's what I mean when I say that the differences in our childhoods are less important than the similarities; none of us escaped the assumption that we would grow up to take care of others, that we are all *by our very natures* disposed to a life at home. It's the same assumption that is made in the Arab countries where I do much of my business. But there, it's assumed to a much more pronounced degree.

It's common knowledge, for example, that the concept of working outside the home is unknown to most Arab women.

So I expected the first time I visited Dubai that I would encounter few if any female office workers. And sure enough, except for foreign women working for foreign firms, there were no female secretaries, no female receptionists, no female clerks, and, of course, no female executives. But I had anticipated this, and I was able to avoid showing surprise the first time I handed my card to a male receptionist.

What did surprise me, though, was my first visit to a large, local restaurant. There was a lot of gaping and gasping as I was brought to my table. Conversation, which can grow quite heated and still remain friendly in the Arab countries, ceased at every table I passed. I was aware of heads swiveling to gawk at me. Naturally, I assumed that it was my Western style of dress that warranted all this attention.

It wasn't until I had settled myself and ascertained that the waiter could translate for me that I got my shock. I looked around the room, and it dawned on me that all the other patrons were men. There wasn't one woman in the place. It wasn't until I asked my waiter to explain that I began to understand how totally circumscribed and homebound by their culture are Arab women. It's a fact that women in some of the Arab societies are not allowed even the modest freedom of taking a meal outside the home. I'm sure that even the most conservative of American men would regard that as extreme.

• *Programmed as "Helpers"* •

What we must understand, however, is that the *underlying* programming of women in the Arab culture (and many other foreign cultures as well) is really quite similar to what goes on here. That's the core common to all of us: every one of us women, regardless of our superficial differences, was prepared to a greater or lesser degree to be a wife, mother, and homemaker. Every one of us was programmed, in other words, to be a helper exclusively, to fulfill a function that is by its nature supportive and subsidiary.

Now, please don't take these remarks as an attack on motherhood. And if you do, don't tell my sons. I respect and admire

6

the career of homemaker. Besides, who else should be a mother but a woman? The role of wife and mother is honorable and intrinsically rewarding. Clearly, what is offensive is not the role of homemaker itself but the programming that virtually ignores preparing us for anything else.

Such social programming isn't necessarily malicious, either, and I don't mean to suggest otherwise. In fact, programming of our everyday behavior patterns is actually a necessary task of society; our culture couldn't function without it. But in this case, it's too restrictive. It doesn't allow for possibilities in addition to the homemaking role.

Does it make sense, for example, to treat our daughters as if the homemaking career were *inevitable*? The right of today's woman to maximize her achievement in the workplace is insured by law. That causes some women to choose to make their careers outside the home. Although that choice often implies a corresponding and detrimental impact on family life, it's a choice we've been guaranteed by our laws, and those laws must be respected. Even those of us who prefer to enjoy the conventional homemaking role in the traditional nuclear family setting typically work for a period—often an *extended* period—before marriage or before starting a family. My point is that whether we choose either a permanent career outside the home or a temporary job until the baby comes, most of us women will certainly spend enough time in the working world that our early programming should include some recognition of the need to prepare for it.

And does it make sense to treat our daughters as if the homemaking career were *exclusive*? Statistics show that most of us mothers are now required by economic circumstance to work outside the home in addition to raising our families. The archetypal "Leave It to Beaver" nuclear family, which has a father working outside the home and a mother working inside the home, seems to be going the way of the passenger pigeon under contemporary pressures. It has been my experience that far too many women are ill-prepared for the dual role of mother and worker, both parts of which are important to the complete modern woman.

7

Further, does it make sense to treat our daughters as if the homemaking career were *forever*? In an era when statistics tell us that more than half of all marriages dissolve, that's a very dangerous assumption for a group of people who have a good chance of becoming working single parents. But even more to the point, there's another consideration that applies to every last one of us women, including those who will never have to face the hardship of raising children without help. Even if all goes beautifully in your life and you're blessed with a firm marriage and wonderful, healthy kids, your mothering career nevertheless terminates when your youngsters grow up. *You,* of course, are still young and productive when that happens. So what will you do for an encore when you're only forty-five or so?

• *The Problems with Our Programming* •

It's those three assumptions built into our early programming—the assumptions that the homemaker role is inevitable, exclusive, and forever—that create the problem. It's a problem that's easy to see, once you know to look for it: we get the idea that orienting our daughters toward a life in the world is less important than orienting them toward a life in the home. *And it's wrong to ignore either aspect of life at the expense of the other.* Doing so tends to produce women who have trouble dealing with both aspects of life, particularly the working aspect. These are the women who exhibit in the workplace the unconscious programmed behavior that more properly belongs to the sensitive, nurturing, caring homemaker role. These are the women who self-destruct.

We become lopsided when homemaking behavior is the only kind for which we've been programmed, when we've been taught only one set of responses to the world's challenges. As the old saying has it, "When the only tool you've got is a hammer, everything starts to look like a nail." Just so, we women will respond with the only tools we've got whether the response is appropriate or not. We act as we've been programmed to act.

Preparing our daughters for serious, permanent careers, in other words, remains the exception rather than the rule. And if you're one of the many who received insufficient orientation in your childhood toward the possibility of a career other than homemaker, you've been shortchanged by the kind of inadequate early programming we're talking about.

It's the subtlety of that programming that causes all the trouble. It's the fact that you might never think about why you're different unless somebody points it out to you specifically. It's like walking around with a Kick Me sign on your back and, since you can't see it, wondering why everybody's kicking you. The first thing you need to do is what this chapter's all about: find out you've got a sign back there. And once you find out the sign is back there, you begin to understand why you've been kicked around so much.

If I had to summarize the effect of this programming on us women in one phrase, I would say that it has caused us to appear to emphasize relational values above all others. An excessive emphasis on relational values would explain much of our behavior both on and off the job.

Consider, for example, that many of us women who work need to get rewards in addition to money from our jobs. To be sure, we want and need the income that working brings. But many of us are motivated by more than sales, wealth, and power. We're motivated also by the human values that we get from our work, values such as the friendship of our coworkers and expressions of need for our help and of approval for good work.

These different motivations toward our work lead to a set of measurements by which we gauge our success that's different from the set used by most men. Therefore, the woman who counts herself as successful because she gets along well with her boss and with the others, has a cheery disposition, and keeps a neat desk is surprised when she's kicked by a negative performance appraisal. She may have been counting as too important some of the things that are peripheral to why her employer wants her there. Getting along, being cheery, and keeping the place neat probably aren't what her job is *about*. Yet they occupy a primary place in her priorities because they emphasize the qualities she's been programmed to appreciate. Unfortunately for her, they may occupy a subordinate place in her employer's priorities.

It's not that relational values are trivial in business. It's just that they can be thought of as only one of several balls that all businesses must juggle constantly. There are lots of other balls that have to be kept in the air in addition to the "relational values" ball.

Only one of those balls is bright red. It's the one labeled *"Profit."* The reason you and all women haven't gotten ahead far enough, fast enough is business's fear that, because of your obsession with the "relational values" ball, you might drop the red ball. And in business you must never, never drop the red ball—or even give the impression that you might. Any behavior that gives business the opinion, however erroneous, that you might even for an instant take your eye off the red ball is your enemy. It will be used against you (and against all the rest of us as well) by those who are unscrupulous.

So watch it. They're waiting for you to appear unable to make objective judgments, to seem to be "emotional" (which is to say, too strongly concerned with human values).

Relational values assign much importance to persons and relatively little importance to property. Consequently, they're not the kinds of things that business is *about,* strictly speaking, because the function of business is (and must be) the increase of property.

All of that is not to say that human values are without worth to business or that they have no place in business. My personal belief, in fact, is that few businesses could fail to improve from an injection of the moral and emotional sensitivity that women, because of our early programming, bring to the workplace.

Indeed, the human values to which our early programming has made us women so sensitive have enormous positive implications for business. That is, many of the virtues instilled by our programming can be valuable not only in family life, but in our working lives as well. For example, the frugality with which most women are taught to run their households is much esteemed in business. Of course, in business we call it "cost consciousness," but the principle is the same.

• *The Conflict* •

Behavior learned early in life can be detrimental later on when you go to work for a living, if you remain unaware of how you were trained. Many of us were programmed *exclusively* with the attitudes, habits, and characteristics needed for the motherhood role. While they are often the very same attitudes, habits, and characteristics that are related to success in the business world, this isn't always the case.

Sometimes, in other words, our values are in conflict. Consider, for example, our need for security. Everyone will agree that security should be of paramount concern to a mother responsible for young children. But that concern just naturally makes her cautious. Success in the business world, by comparison, usually requires a willingness to assume a prudent degree of risk. So the stronger a woman's sensitivity to security, the more she is likely to be a dutiful mother, other things being equal. But she's also less likely to take chances, and this hurts her in the workplace, no matter whether she's the lowest worker or the highest boss.

That need-for-security characteristic may show up on a performance review in such a form as: "She fails to demonstrate the initiative necessary to justify promotion," which is the kind of innocuous-sounding remark that tends in reality to be a career killer. Here, the value a mother properly places on clutching security is in conflict with the value a business places on assuming prudent risk.

It's this kind of conflict in programmed values that leads you to exhibit behaviors harmful to women who work. These are only a small portion of your entire behavior repertoire, of course, so your learning to stop committing them involves distinguishing those habits that are detrimental to your success at work from the others that resulted from your programming. To use a motherly expression, you'll want to avoid "throwing out the baby with the bath water" when you try to isolate and eliminate your mistakes and to begin giving the working world a more favorable impression of yourself.

I've been using words like *impression, appear,* and *seem* all along. I don't mean to make business's reaction to you seem as superficial as those words might imply. And yet I want you to understand that you've been conditioned to merely *appear* to be wrong for work. That you've been conditioned to *appear* passive, yielding, and noncompetitive. That you've been conditioned to *appear* to be considerate of human values to the exclusion of all others, even when you're paid to consider other needs of business ahead of them. I've stressed the word *appear* because of what early programming has done to the way you appear to business through your job habits. If your habits are appropriate to some place other than the workplace, they will probably not be conducive to your business success. And your programmers want you to *appear* to be inappropriate for business.

• *Programming Rules Behavior* •

Thus, one of the things we're going to be most concerned with in this book is habits that produce behavior that lets people focus on how you as a woman are *different*. Again, this is behavior you exhibit without thinking about it. Behavior you don't even notice you're displaying. Behavior that's often small and seemingly inconsequential. Behavior resulting from the early programming that turned you into a woman.

But there's one really good thing about bad habits. They can be broken.

The rest of this book calls to your attention some of the more common of these habits in the belief that once you become aware of them, you're more likely to break them. We'll be talking about the habits themselves and not whether they're universal; you as an individual may not possess some of them. That means I'll be using some stereotypes about women in general as if they were accurate reflections of how *all* women really are. You might balk at some of those stereotypes because you feel they're overgeneralizations or offensive or just plain inaccurate. But your opinion of the accuracy of these stereotypes isn't important for the purposes of our discussion. What *is* important is *what male-dominated business can get away with thinking about you when you exhibit job behavior that it regards as inappropriate.* I therefore suggest you pretend these stereotypes of female behavior are accurate portrayals even if just "for the sake of discussion," okay?

I hope you're not offended by anything that follows, but I'd rather see you offended than see you help yourself get kicked around some more.

CHAPTER 2

Choosing a Challenging Job

My friend Margie was the most intellectually gifted person I've ever known. She got straight A's all through school, was editor of the school paper, state chess champion—you name it. If people usually said something required "smarts," Margie was a whiz at it.

After school, we both decided to build business careers for ourselves. I felt that the choices open to us women were so limited in those days that I really didn't have much to lose. So I learned to take a lot of chances with my career.

Margie, on the other hand, played it conservatively. Her new college degree notwithstanding, she accepted a job as a trainee typist at a large downtown bank. I remember I was appalled when she told me of her decision. I knew she could have done jobs that would let her stretch well beyond the one she took.

Margie explained her decision with words like "safe" and "secure." In fact, she went further than simply trying to justify her own decision. She counseled me to straighten out and follow her example before I got involved in some kind of fierce, competitive business where the sharks would try to eat me alive.

There were times when I felt that Margie knew what she was talking about. But most times, it seemed to me that her choice made for a limited kind of working life—not bad or unpleasant, you understand, but less challenging than her gifts would have allowed her to experience.

She was thoroughly loyal to the bank, of course. One of the many signs of dedication she displayed, for example, was that she took time off over the years only to have her children. Both times, she took a couple of months, and then it was right back into harness at the good old bank. She never made much money there, but I have to admit it surely was solid.

Notice that I said it *was* solid. A couple of years ago, the place nearly went broke. You probably read about it; it was in all the papers. One of the things they did in response to the crisis was to lay off people like Margie—people who made a higher than competitive salary because of long tenure, but who were thought to be too old to be of any great value to the bank's future.

There's no dramatic ending to Margie's story. She didn't have to declare bankruptcy or lose her house or anything like that. She even found another job—typing shipping labels for a mail order house.

• *Playing It Safe* •

The real point of Margie's story is that total job security is an illusion. Most jobs are "terminable at will," and the employment application you signed when you accepted your present job probably included a statement to that effect. Too bad it was in small print, because it makes a wonderful reminder that you don't own your job.

This is especially true of jobs that are traditionally thought of as "women's work." Make no mistake—the more women there are in your line of work, the more expendable you are. After all, lots of companies still don't think of us as "breadwinners." They still regard us as the earners of "supplemental family income," even though the number of families headed by single heads of households (usually women) increases in every census.

15

In other words, if you think you're buying job security by taking one of the "safe" jobs that seem to be done mostly by women, you may want to think again. Being a nurse or a teacher or a secretary can be a wonderful career. But you ought to have better reasons for choosing one of those jobs than believing you'll be insulated from the competitive demands of the working world.

The freedom of us women to choose any job we want has only recently been acknowledged. But many of us shy away from that freedom as if it were frightening rather than liberating. Many of us continue to accept work that's comfortable, familiar, and friendly, seeming to prefer the subservience of inferior roles to the responsibility of the more competitive world. We continue to choose the "safe and secure" occupations we've been programmed to choose in spite of having become better educated to our own possibilities and in spite of the laws that guarantee our opportunity.

We continue to allow ourselves to be re-enslaved, in a manner of speaking. We allow this not because we're stupid or lazy but because human nature always tries to reassert itself. And human nature prefers comfort to hardship; it prefers the known to the unknown. So, to most of us, fulfilling the stereotypically subordinate female role in the workplace is preferable to challenging the system and breaking new career ground. It's an outlook that holds us all back. It goes far in explaining why we haven't gotten as far ahead in business as fast as we should have.

• *The Wrong Career Choices* •

That outlook causes us to make three wrong choices about our jobs: it leads us to choose the wrong *type* of work, the wrong *level* of work, and the wrong *employer*.

Consider the *types* of work that are favored by women. Because we're programmed to be supportive and caring, we tend to choose the "helping" or "nurturing" careers; teaching and medical work, for example. We've also been programmed to appreciate attractiveness, so we aspire to "glamour" jobs in travel or fashion. And even those of us in the pecuniary world of pure commerce seem to concentrate ourselves in "people-oriented" areas such as "the three P's": purchasing, public relations, and personnel. We also congregate around the careers, such as publishing and design, that are thought to be somehow more genteel and more sensitive, that have a "higher value." It's another manifestation of the early programming that makes us like to stay "clean" psychologically as well as physically. We therefore avoid the "scut" jobs in life, opting out of work where we can't have a bud vase on the desk.

Those were nasty remarks, I admit. But remember that the way you perceive yourself and other women in the workplace is not important for the purposes of our discussion. What *is* important is *how you are perceived*. And business perceives women in general to be fussy. As one of my male clients reminded me during our interview, the term *prima donna,* which we all understand to refer to a vain and overly sensitive person, was originally a term used in opera and always refers to a woman. So please don't be offended if the remarks above seem unfair or excessive.

Besides, there's worse to come.

In addition to voluntarily limiting ourselves mostly to "female" types of work, we often settle for a *level* of work that's too low. We don't shoot high enough. The result is that even though there are *some* women at work in all the most important and powerful levels of all professions, we represent about 100 percent of the supportive ranks in those same professions. That is, we tend to permit ourselves to become nurses rather than doctors, paralegals rather than lawyers, hygienists rather than dentists, cabin attendants rather than pilots, and secretaries rather than executives.

Incidentally, my personnel company has recruited an enormous number of office workers—mostly secretaries for the executives we recruit—over the years. It gives me, I think, a unique perspective on the attitudes that rule women who work in offices. That means I may use a lot of examples based on office work. That's okay because the "female ghetto" is not a place, it's a state of mind. So the problems we women create

17

for ourselves by voluntarily occupying our ghettos are the same whether our ghettos are in an office, a classroom, or the great outdoors. That allows office examples to serve as well as any others. And besides, our third big mistake draws us to office work in droves. More of us do office work than any other kind.

That third big mistake is another result of our preference for choosing that which has been chosen before. Even though we're free to consider any type of work and any level of work, we still tend to choose the wrong *employer*. We prefer to work in those industries and for those specific employers that have gained a reputation for being "friendly." We favor those industries and employers that have already demonstrated they accept the idea of women as workers. Consequently, these industries, such as education and banking, tend to attract disproportionate numbers of women to their ranks. That's one of the many reasons we earn less than we should.

All those restrictions we impose on ourselves about the type of work we choose, the level of work we accept, and the employers we approach are what I have in mind when I say that we women are too traditional in all aspects of our career choices. The responsibility that goes with our new freedom requires that we blaze some new trails for our daughters. It requires that we go "where we aren't wanted" instead of staying "in our place." It requires that we break out of the ghetto. But that hasn't happened enough yet. Too often we have tended to take the comfortable path, the one that's well-worn by the women who preceded us.

• *The Best Example: Secretarial Work* •

One very well-worn path is that of the secretary. It's the best "job as ghetto" example of which I'm aware. And yet it never should have happened that only women go down that path. The phenomenon is so peculiar that I sometimes refer to it as "The Strange Case of the Female Secretary."

You might not think there's anything peculiar about a secretary's being female, because you've probably never encountered any other kind. But female domination of the secretarial profession was so unlikely around the turn of the century that a businessman would have laughed at you had you suggested it. Completely contrary to today, the secretarial occupation was at that time an exclusively male province. I have always been astonished not only at how quickly the situation reversed, but also at how completely. If you're one of the many, many secretaries who don't know how their profession came to be the way it is, you might find the story interesting.

As with many of our English words, *secretary* comes from a Latin word. The Latin language classified nouns ending in *-us* as masculine in gender. And the Latin word from which we got *secretary* was *secretarius,* a masculine noun, establishing the nature of the profession as the Romans saw it. It was considered, in other words, to be a male job involving acting as the boss's *alter ego,* his delegate, his viceroy. It was an exalted position below only that of the boss himself. About the only place where this meaning of the word persists today is in government, where the heads of departments in the executive branch are still known as the Secretary of State, the Secretary of Defense, and so on.

Knowing that the original Latin word meant "a confidential employee" may help explain why women were never considered as possible secretaries: because principals in a business were until recently almost always men, would you expect them to willingly divulge their *secrets,* their confidential business matters, to a female? Their sense of masculine prerogatives precluded entrusting women with this very important job. Accordingly, secretaries were always men, even from ancient times.

What happened to change this is that around the turn of the century, transcribing written material with a typewriter became an important part of the secretarial job—so much so, in fact, that being privy to the boss's business secrets and filling in for him became secondary to typing. Eventually, being the boss's surrogate all but disappeared as a job requirement. The preeminence of the typing skill in the secretarial job continues even to the present day, when many women having the title "secretary" should really be called "typist."

At first, the introduction of the typewriter made little difference to the male bastion of secretaryship. Christopher Sholes, inventor of the typewriter, argued against the use of his device by women, saying, "The rigors of typewriting machine operation well exceed the physical capacities of the fairer gender." If you've ever seen some of those early "typewriting machines," you might conclude that Mr. Sholes wasn't as sexist as that remark makes him sound. What clunkers they were!

But as technology improved those monsters, and as our economy became increasingly paper-intensive, requiring more office labor, women inevitably began to be tapped as a resource. As more women came into the secretarial ranks, male bosses downgraded the importance of the job. Over time, this position—once the second most important in any business, you'll recall—declined in status. The decline continues to this day so that we find in the same Merriam Webster dictionary from which I got the Latin etymology this definition of the word *secretary:* "One employed to handle the correspondence and manage *routine and detail work for a superior*" (emphasis added).

The definition above demonstrates the extent to which the secretarial profession is a subordinate or a "helping" position in the eyes of the general public. And although the story I've just told you is about secretaries, it could as easily have been about nursing (a male business until Florence Nightingale), teaching (a male business until there was a shortage of educated men in newly civilized America), and the other careers dominated by women. So if I use the secretarial position to make a point more frequently than you'd like, remember that we could just as easily have used any other female occupation.

The point is that the occupations preferred by females are the "helping" kinds of careers. And we overwhelm those careers with our numbers. Sadly, we women take to careers the way blackbirds take to the fence rail: when one comes to sit there, they *all* come to sit there. And when one flies away, they *all* fly away.

Nothing leads me to believe that this situation will change soon. A recent piece of research prepared by my staff (*Profile of an Executive Secretary,* I. D. I., 1986) was about attitudes.

But we discovered something interesting quite by accident. It had to do not with the responses to our questionnaire but rather with the *names* on the list we used to mail it out. This is how it happened: we intended to mail one type of questionnaire to 576 top executives in Chicago and a different type to their 576 secretaries. We discovered when making up the list that a few of the top executives were female: one runs a cosmetics firm, two were in consulting, one was in advertising/public relations, two were in architecture/design, and three others were prominent lawyers.

But all the secretaries on our list turned out to be female, so far as we could tell from their names.

Why this is so peculiar is that these secretaries make good money; the average was over $25,000. You would think that a profession like this one where incumbents are in the top half of all wage earners would be attractive to men as well as women. But not a single male secretary could we find. It appears that this profession will be a female preserve for the foreseeable future.

• *Women Who Run the Business* •

If we women are too traditional in our career choices when we work for somebody else, surely we're innovative when we work for ourselves, right? Wrong. Our excessive traditionalism in our career choices holds true even for the most dynamic and the most successful among us: we who start our own businesses, the entrepreneurs.

Consider two of the premier businesswomen in America, Mary Kay Ash and Debbi Fields. Their names ought to be on the tip of your tongue if you're interested in women and their work, although there's a good chance that you won't be able to identify them immediately. That's because the names of women don't spring to mind when we discuss great business entrepreneurs. We simply don't think of women in that role. This amnesia is justified by the scarcity of female business owners, which is especially severe because entrepreneurship has always been the American escape route for classes of people who have been objects of economic discrimination. When we Americans are maltreated by those who employ us, we tend to start our own businesses and employ ourselves. But two barriers that result from our early programming prohibit women's full use of this escape route.

One reason we don't start our own businesses often enough is that our need for security implanted by our early programming is so great as to prevent it. We simply don't roll the dice as often as we should. It's not that we're incapable of generating moneymaking ideas, it's just that we sit on our hands and fail by default. We watch our own brilliance turned into profit by those with more tolerance for risk. As Emerson said, "In every work of genius, we recognize our own rejected thoughts."

It's easy to confirm our reticence to assume risk. Just ask any commercial loan officer how many women come in for commercial loans—not *personal* loans, but *commercial* loans, the kind that support business activities. Ask any venture capitalist how many women look for meaningful start-up capital—not "chump change," but "megabucks," to use the jargon of that industry. Ask any investment banker how many women build a company to the point that it can be taken public through a stock sale.

And if you don't know any commercial bankers, venture capitalists, or investment bankers, then ask yourself how many famous female entrepreneurs you can name. Oh, sure, you can now name Mary Kay Ash, the founder of Mary Kay Cosmetics, and Debbi Fields, who started Mrs. Fields' Cookies, since I just mentioned them. But what can you do for an encore?

These women are both brilliant. After having read their books and articles, I'm absolutely convinced that either of them could have used her genius to make a fortune in any business she chose to favor with her participation.

So why cosmetics? Why cookies?

Because they're women. Just like you and me, these outstanding women were conditioned by early programming. When their entrepreneurial bumps started to itch, they just naturally turned to their own experiences for a business, so they wound up doing cosmetics and cookies. Great cosmetics and super cookies, to be sure. But not steel mills or shipping companies or computer manufacturing or investment banking houses.

Cosmetics and cookies. It's what we do because it's what we've been programmed for.

But we must break out of the cosmetic and cookie ghetto. It's an obligation to future generations that faces each of us. In other words, each of us women must face up to the responsibility of being successful, and we can do it in lots of areas other than the traditional ones.

I know that many women will object to my statements to the effect that we don't amount to much as entrepreneurs. So I did a little research based on the 1982 U.S. Census to see whether I could substantiate the point. I found that we women own nearly 3 million small businesses. A friend of mine immediately pointed out that that was pretty good. In fact, it's nearly a quarter of all the small businesses operating in America today, up from less than 20 percent ten years ago. My friend contends that it represents good progress. He's right, of course. But before we congratulate ourselves on having become so independent, let's notice that we're still only a third as likely to go out on our own as are men.

Further interpretation of those census data suggests that almost all our businesses (about 92 percent) are the form of enterprise known as the proprietorship (a business owned by one person). The proprietorship form typically accounts for the very smallest of small business. It suggests that we women don't make much money from our own businesses, even when we find ourselves courageous and determined enough to start them. To verify the suspicion, let's look at the income figures for our businesses in the same census data.

About half of all female-owned businesses had gross annual revenues of less than $5,000. Read that again—that's *gross* revenue! You can imagine what the *net* (or "take-home") is. How serious can we be about our own businesses when the majority of them earn us less than would the minimum wage? And as for the "big" small businesses, those grossing one million dollars or more a year, only about one-fourth of 1 percent of all female-owned companies qualify. Even including those few "big" businesses run by women doesn't change the figures much for overall calculations: our full quarter of all American businesses accounted for only about a tenth of all the receipts.

The data also shed light on the *kinds* of businesses we start. The businesses most frequently owned by women are in the personal service field: laundry and dry cleaning shops, beauty shops, child-care services, and so forth. Real estate sales agencies were second. (The residential side of real estate is dominated by female salespeople and female-owned firms, although we're underrepresented on the commercial side.) The health services ranked third in number of woman-owned businesses. It seems that even when we start businesses, we tend toward the nurturing, "home-and-health" types of enterprise.

But there are so many other possibilities in business. It's not that the other facets of your life are more important than your female propensity to be a caring person and to reflect that caring in your work; that's not the message at all. It's just that there are aspects to you *in addition* to your programmed "home and help" tendencies. Let them come out. I can assure you from my personal experience that the rewards (financial and psychological) that come with being a pioneer, a groundbreaker, are great. In other words, you'll make more money *and* you'll have more fun.

Refuse to let your early programming limit you. Let yourself take prudent risks with your career. We all tend to overestimate the amount of courage we need to break out and be pathfinders. I promise you this about taking a career risk: once you've done it, you'll wonder why you waited so long.

And when I tell you to be a pathfinder, a pioneer, a groundbreaker, I'm not talking only to those who want to be executives like corporate presidents, those who like to assume risk like entrepreneurs, or those who aspire to the most demanding professions like airline pilots. Those of us who do the world's daily work need to break out, too. We need to become the supermarket managers as well as the checkers. We need to become, in greater numbers than now, the auto salespeople, the firefighters, the sanitation workers, and the electricians that our nation has guaranteed us we can be. As well as becoming the corporate presidents, the entrepreneurs, and the airline pilots, of course.

Our early programming, however, prevents most of us from getting a good start on all that "becoming." It induces in us a peculiar sort of egomania that's the subject of the next chapter. It originates in the hurt we feel being second-class citizens in third-class jobs. It's extremely harmful to the woman who works, because it can manifest itself in the form of hostility toward those to whom we report.

If you suffer from this condition of the ego, it's your assurance that, once you start near the bottom, you'll tend to stay there. The cure is to recognize the condition and break the habits that cause you to exhibit the next error, failing to cope with your ego.

CHAPTER 3

Controlling the Ego

I'm in the habit of telling stories about the women who have worked for my personnel business over the years. Some would say all that reminiscing is a sign of advancing age. But I like to think it's a sign that I've been fortunate to know a lot of fascinating people during my career. And many of them have been women, because personnel consulting is one of those female-dominated businesses we just examined.

But sometimes my stories make people think that every woman who ever worked for me automatically had a fulfilling, financially rewarding career. Most did, too, except for one woman who stands out particularly in my mind. So, just to keep everything level, let me tell you about Lucille, a woman who never established herself as a success in business, although she certainly had what it takes.

In fact, Lucille had it *all:* intelligence, drive, good looks, poise. I thought when I hired her that she'd turn out to be a world-beater. Not only did she fail to place new business, however, but an account that we gave her to help her get started also canceled after only a few weeks of Lucille's stewardship. After a couple of months of such disappointing results, I decided to accompany her on a sales call to see what she might be doing wrong.

The client was the personnel director of a famous research lab with strikingly attractive quarters in the suburbs. I recall that as we pulled up, Lucille seemed almost intimidated by the grandeur of the lab's architecture in its magnificent, wooded setting.

After introducing me to the client, Lucille spent several minutes doing what I can only call "showing off." She managed to steer the conversation—not very subtly, I might add—to her designer suit, to her imported car that we'd just parked in the company's lot, and then to her fashionable, "Gold Coast" address.

I was astonished to hear her go on this way. She seemed to be trying to augment her worth as a person by bragging about her possessions. The client's face got steadily stonier as I slunk slowly deeper into my chair. I wrote her arrogant behavior off to being nervous; after all, her boss was observing her. Still, I wished we'd been sitting at a table so I could have kicked her under it.

After a mercifully brief period, the client escorted us out of his office for a tour through the facility. Every time the client began to explain a different functional area, Lucille would ask him how long it would take him to hire somebody to manage it should an opening come up. In one case, I remember he replied, "Six weeks." Lucille said, "I can do it in four." In another case he said, "About a month." She said, "I can do it in two weeks."

It was like watching "Name That Tune."

Finally, with the air of a man trying to escape from an unpleasant conversation, he jokingly said, "I suppose I understand my own job better than any other one in our company. Because if I had to replace myself, I know it would only take me two days."

"Well," Lucille snapped, "I can do it in one!"

We didn't get their business. In fact, we very narrowly escaped being thrown out.

• *Contemporary Programming* •

Lucille had become a victim of her own ego. She had come to regard more highly the outward signs of success than the internal satisfaction of a job well done, to value praise above respect. She had developed the kind of ego that's being constructed in more and more modern women by a new kind of programming. I call it *contemporary* programming as contrasted with the early programming about which we've been talking in previous chapters. It's different from our early programming in the sense that our early programming tried to preclude a successful working life outside the home, whereas this contemporary programming *demands* a successful working life outside the home.

The popular books, the movies, and the TV shows that strongly influence us adult women portray only successful women and emphasize their symbols of success. I mean, just look at the clothes on "Dallas"; superglitz and megabucks, right? These programs magnify the natural avarice that's already in each of us. Also, we're affected by all the books on business success for women; there are so many that, if you could afford to buy them all, you wouldn't *need* business success. And the articles in magazines directed toward women concentrate so much on career success that the woman who's not at the absolute top in her working life actually feels guilty about it.

All this artful propaganda is influential on us women. We begin to think only about how terrific business is at the top and to ignore all the intermediate steps that are needed to get there. We start to think to ourselves, *I want it all, and I want it now.*

This attitude can cause the woman who works to become so wrapped up in her ego needs that she becomes defensive about her status. When this is carried far enough, she even begins to appear hostile. But the way to get ahead involves helping one's employer to get ahead. That requires cooperation rather than confrontation. In fact, nothing is so toxic to success as is hostility to one's employer. That's why the hostility resulting from an uncontrolled ego is a fatal error.

The reason we make this error involves another of those stereotypes that I warned I'd ask you to accept. I admit that it's an uncomfortable observation about the woman who works, but I really believe it's true. The modern American woman who works is confused. She's confused as a result of the inner conflict between the supportiveness required by her early "homemaker programming" and the independence demanded by her contemporary "success programming."

But why should there be a problem? The modern woman might seem at first glance to have it made. Isn't this the age of opportunity, of getting ahead as far and as fast as you can? What does she have to fear? Isn't she free to participate in the great adventure of competing in the workplace?

Yes. And that freedom to compete and excel is at the heart of the problem. The woman who works is beginning to understand that there's something wrong with the heavy emphasis she's been convinced to place on her career and her lifestyle. She knows she's expected to perform, to achieve. And she can sense that she's not been given all that she needs to fulfill that expectation.

Her early programming has tried to make her pliable, dependent, and submissive—characteristics not conducive to moving ahead in the working world. It's made her limit herself by choosing the type of work that emphasizes her supportive, maternal nature. It's made her settle for the types of jobs that are subordinate by nature and that assure her permanent corporate inferiority. It's made her take shelter in industries that are already so crowded with other desperate women that the oversupply precludes any improvement in the abuse we suffer in common.

Yet, our present culture seems to demand that she get ahead equally and immediately.

How can we pretend to be surprised that the woman who works fears this conflict between what she's been made to expect of herself and what she thinks she's been given the tools to do? And how is it that such a conflict came about?

• *Our Changing Expectations* •

What happened is that we women widened our horizons and changed our role expectations. We changed our expectations so quickly, in fact, that our social programming couldn't keep up. Although sociologists might argue interminably about when the change started, it seems to me reasonable to date it to World War II, when we women found (often to our own surprise) that we could do any job a man could do.

After the war, Rosie the Riveter was understandably reluctant to give up her newfound self-esteem. She'd had the rewarding experience of finding herself to be a capable, self-sufficient person. Like all oppressed people who get a taste of liberty, she vowed that the next generation would see still better days. Rosie the Riveter determined that her daughter would be Elizabeth the Executive.

I was a little girl at that time, but I well remember my mother's first working experience. Mother had been schooled in all the "feminine" virtues. Not only was she a good cook and housekeeper, but she'd also studied art and music extensively. She was a graduate of the Juilliard School in New York and had even had a very modest success as a concert pianist before she married. Of course, she considered any sort of work outside the home after marriage as "not fitting." She even declined to give piano lessons.

Beyond her undeniable skill at making a home, at music, and in art, she was totally untrained. She considered herself to be very delicate and took pride in seeming helpless. She might have qualified as an antebellum southern debutante, the model for Scarlett O'Hara, except that she came from Boston.

Those of us who didn't live through the Second World War as adults can only imagine what work must have been like: no such thing as unemployment; three shifts a day at every defense plant, and that not enough. So new plants were built almost overnight. One of them was an aircraft parts plant at what is now O'Hare Airport in Chicago. We lived near the site, and it seemed to me as a child that one day there was a vacant lot, and the next day a massive, smoking factory was there. A big sign out front showed a painting of a stern Uncle Sam pointing at anybody walking by and saying, "I Want *You*."

I suppose Uncle Sam glaring down at her every day made my mother feel guilty, because a few weeks after the plant opened, she announced that it was her patriotic duty to help with the war effort. She said she was going to get a job at the new plant.

My father stopped chewing his meat loaf and stared at her. "You don't know how to do anything," he said.

Mother looked a little confused. "Well, they say they need *everybody*," she said. "They say they can use *any* skills."

My father laughed. "So what job will you apply for? Concert pianist? Maybe they can pipe you over the loudspeakers."

But to her credit, my mother refused to be deterred and marched over to the employment office the next morning. When her time came to be interviewed, she got very nervous. Almost everybody does during an interview, and, even more upsetting, she was a grown woman applying for her first real job.

Besides all that, it suddenly occurred to her that my father was right—she really *didn't* know how to do anything. By the time the personnel man sat her down, she was so nervous that she could barely remember her own name.

"What job are you applying for?" he asked.

"Pianist," she blurted out without thinking.

The man smiled. After you've been a personnel interviewer for a while, nothing people say surprises you any more.

"Lady," he said, "this is a defense plant. We don't need a pianist."

"I'm . . . I'm a very *good* pianist," she said, shredding up the Kleenex she clutched in her lap.

"I'm sure you are. But what we need right now is machinists. I don't suppose. . . . No, I guess not. Well, do you think you could learn to operate a rivet gun?"

Mother must have looked horrified at the thought of operating any sort of gun.

"Okay, lady, don't get nervous. We also need drivers to move material around. Can you drive?"

Mother shook her head.

"That's okay. We need office workers, too. Can you type?"

Mother shook her head again and piled more Kleenex on the man's floor.

"How about shorthand? bookkeeping? switchboard? filing?"

More shaking and more piling.

"Do you have any experience as a receptionist? or as a messenger?"

Mother looked as if she were about to cry.

"Hmm, there must be something. . . . Look, we need everybody to help with the war effort. Now, I don't know what you're suited for, but we'll find out; we have some tests. In the meantime, I'm putting you on the payroll, and you can go sit in the typing pool.

"But don't volunteer for a typing assignment," he added as an afterthought.

For a month, Mother sat with the typing pool, waiting for her tests. Because she had nothing to do, she started to help divide the work evenly among the typists. She began to check on the quality of the work and to ascertain who was having problems keeping up. When one of the typists was injured in the plant, Mother got all the appropriate forms and helped the girl fill them out. She volunteered to coordinate the War Bond sales drive, the Red Cross training exercises, the Civil Defense plan, and everything else that needed doing and didn't appear to fall within anybody else's assigned duties.

By the time the promised aptitude tests arrived, she was already the de facto head of the typing pool for the entire plant complex. Those who had gotten used to reporting to her virtually insisted that the position be made official. It was the start of a career in office management that she couldn't give up even after the war.

Now, remember that management jobs were pretty much off limits to women back then, even jobs managing departments that were populated exclusively by other women. But Mother ultimately wound up almost running the gigantic old Edgewater Beach Hotel in Chicago before it became a condominium complex. And getting that very first job, liking it, and finding her success at it built an attitude that led her to help me start confidently on the road to my own success.

Of course, this isn't to say that she wanted me to succeed in preference to my brother or that she wanted my brother to be a loser at life. On the contrary, what she stressed was the same "equality" of opportunity regardless of sex that we women want for both our daughters *and* our sons.

• *Success Obsession* •

Because of the emphasis we've learned to place on achievement for *all* our children, today's young American adults of either sex have grown up in an atmosphere of insistence that they "do better" than their parents. The result is an obsession with career success. The worship of success has become our newest national disease.

Not only are we obsessed with success itself, but we're preoccupied with its outward symbols, too. The advertisers know it and shamelessly (and effectively) exploit our insecurity. For instance, each of us women has been conditioned to insist on having only the most expensive products because "I'm worth it." And we've been taught that we must prove to our friends that we care about them "enough to send the very best."

The push to acquire and to display the symbols of success goes beyond slogans. It makes our consumption behavior radically different from that of previous generations. There was a time when minimizing expenditure was considered far more virtuous than it is today. I remember the first time I got enough money together to last for more than the one week until the next payday. I bought a freezer, one of those big industrial ones, and filled it with as much meat as I could afford—not because I wanted the meat (you can't *wear* meat, after all), but because it was so much cheaper to buy it in bulk. And this kind of creative economy made us feel good, kind of upright and noble.

But not anymore. Now we demand imported cars at four times the price of fully adequate, although rather common, alternatives. We insist on gold watches at a hundred times the price of equally reliable, if somewhat ordinary, timepieces.

This obsession with the bold public display of success is typical of the type of contemporary programming with which we have to contend. The way to sell us something by using this programming is to appeal to our pride, to massage our egos. We've become, to use my mother's term, spoiled rotten, and contemporary programming reinforces that condition. The *symbols* of success have become more important to many of us than the *fact* of success. The more we spend on those symbols, the happier some of us are.

But it's not because the fancier products perform that much better than their more economical competition. It's because Mercedes Benz and Rolex symbolize the achievement of the success with which we are obsessed. We're not buying cars or watches or jeans so much as we're buying an advertisement that tells the world we've achieved the career success others desire. We're buying someone else's envy.

That's not only morally questionable, it's also stupid. There's no way you can have "the best" of possessions; if you ever get "the best," somebody will come up with something better. It's called "progress." To understand the futility of desiring "the best" too strongly, to understand that it is, in the poetry of Ecclesiastes, "vanity and a chase after wind," visit the Middle East.

I suffered from the same condition, the "I want it all and I want it now" disease, until my first trip to Abu Dhabi. By that time, I was able to afford some of those things that we all seem to want so much. And I'll be honest: it felt really good, really "big time," at first. In Abu Dhabi, however, I learned that one of the sheikhs I would ultimately work for was accustomed to buying as birthday presents for his children the same kind of Mercedes for which I'd worked so hard and about which I was so vain. But, of course, each of *their* cars had a driver so the youngsters could be driven around wherever they wanted to go.

Then it got even worse. I learned that these were the cars he would buy for his children of whom he wasn't overly fond. His firstborn son, on the other hand, got a new Rolls Royce every birthday!

Well, it sort of made me think, you know? I mean, no matter how well I could ever show off, there was someone who could show off even better. A whole lot better!

There's a message there that I'd like you to understand fully. The material gains of success are not all they're cracked up to be. Persons of religious faith have always known that and have warned about the folly of greed. Nonreligious philosophers have come to pretty much the same conclusion as well. The business psychologist Abraham Maslow, for instance, proved that money is no incentive to work hard. He found that, above a certain level, additional wages had no persistent effect on a worker's performance.

Yet in spite of our intuitive knowledge of this truth, we modern women have been taught to expect much of ourselves in the sense of achievement. We've also been taught to expect much *for* ourselves in the sense of material rewards. But we've been denied the tools to live up to those expectations. This conflict engenders in us women who work a fear of being thought less than enormously successful at our careers.

• *Fear and Failure* •

Fear makes for a very fragile ego. A frightened woman will try to defend her ego with self-destructive behavior. She takes her resentment out on the company by failing to give whole-hearted performance, by stubbornly resisting goals, by subtly sabotaging objectives, by thinking about her own career path so much that she never gets around to thinking about the company's success path. And because her contemporary programming runs contrary to critical thinking, she never consciously realizes that her behavior is counterproductive.

Like all other creatures, the woman who works has a repertoire of only two possible reactions to fear: fight or flight. But she needs her job for income; flight from it is out of the question.

So she fights. But she has a subordinate, helping type of job, as we saw earlier. Typically, that's not the kind of job that wields much influence or authority. And if she's young, she's probably starting near the bottom, as well. It all means that she is in a relatively powerless position in the workplace.

So she uses the only weapons a powerless person has. She uses what the psychologists call passive-aggressive behavior— "aggressive" implying the combative, militant effect that such behavior has and "passive" implying that goals are accomplished without direct, blameful action. In the everyday language preferred by Mohandas Gandhi, this was "passive resistance" and it was amazingly effective.

A woman's passive-aggressive job behavior involves withholding cooperation from those to whom she reports. Not only can the result be devastating, but the perpetrator can usually cop a plea that she didn't realize how serious the matter was, thus escaping the personal consequences. Let me give you a f'rinstance that clarifies what kind of behavior we're talking about. (See if you know anybody who behaves this way.)

Recently, I was privileged to attend an air show in Europe as the guest of one of the Arab nations. It was the world's biggest aircraft and equipment exposition, a "must" for anyone in the aircraft business, kind of the way the Cannes Film Festival is for people in the movie industry.

During the previous summer in Chicago, I had looked after the son of the Middle Eastern businessman who arranged this air show invitation by his country's air force. When he returned home, the boy, Ashraft, kept up a vigorous correspondence with his new American chum, my son Dwight. So my friend was gracious enough to arrange an invitation for Dwight, too.

Imagine the thrill for a sixteen-year-old. A few days in London to do anything he wanted in the care of an old friend of mine while I tended to some business. Then the air show, followed by a week at a villa on the Costa Smeralda owned by one of the sheikhs for whom I work. His pal Ashraft would be there, too, and the sheikh had promised to let them use his sailboat. Wow! No kid would ever behave in such a way as to jeopardize a trip like that, right?

If that's what you think, you were never sixteen.

Dwight had been feeling resentful toward me. I had "grounded" him a week earlier for having violated his curfew. So he indulged in a little of the passive-aggressive behavior we're talking about. As I was packing his clothes the day before we were to leave, I couldn't find any of his long-sleeve shirts, which I knew he'd need as there would be dinners to attend overseas. But as I looked through his closet, all I saw were short-sleeves, short-sleeves, and more short—

No, wait! They weren't short-sleeved shirts at all. They were no-sleeved shirts! For some reason comprehensible only to a sixteen-year-old mind, Dwight had cut the sleeves off every shirt he owned: dress shirts, sweat shirts, even an authentic Yoruba dashiki I'd bought for him on a trip to Nigeria.

It was the fashion that year for teen-aged boys to wear sleeveless shirts—sleeveless *old* shirts. So Dwight wasn't being deliberately or consciously destructive. He could justify himself by saying that "all the other guys are doing it." Of course, as far as I know, I alone was gifted with a son who cut the sleeves off *all* his shirts.

You can imagine that I was less than overjoyed. I had to dash out to the store and buy him a couple of shirts when I really needed the time to finish packing. So I confronted him. You know what he said to me to justify and defend himself?

"You never told me not to."

I mean, really! The fact is that he was resentful of the confrontation we'd had a week earlier. Being in the powerless position in which young people find themselves, he showed his resentment in this petulant way.

It's the same thing that happens with the young women who resent starting at the bottom on their jobs. It's what happens with all women who work when they have no way to deal with unconscious resentment. And I'm not saying that the resentment is unjustified, either. But justified or not, management winds up feeling the same way about these women that I did about Dwight.

Of course, behavior of this type is seldom as blatant as was Dwight's, because the sanctions can be severe. Thus, it's often so subtle that women may not even realize they're doing it. That makes it a fatal error for a woman who works—behavior harmful to her career that she displays because she's a woman and that she doesn't even realize she's displaying.

Some excellent examples of this kind of destructive behavior were displayed by Heather, a young woman who worked for me briefly some years ago. I met her through a friend who was working with a youth group. My friend sometimes enlists the help of my personnel company to help his kids get ready to find work. His belief—and I share it with him—is that the self-respect that comes with work may be even more important for a young person than is the income. So he does his best to see that every kid he works with finds a job. But Heather, he felt, was a "hopeless case": she was clinically depressed with a history of drug use. She was a dropout with no skills and she was inarticulate, shy, and a bit clumsy besides.

So, naturally, I became a victim once again of the "lost puppy" syndrome. I invented a new job and hired Heather as my "personal executive assistant." She was supposed to help with travel arrangements and things like that so that my secretary (who is outstanding) could take life just a tad easier.

The experiment went poorly from the start. I was able to pay Heather only a bit more than the minimum wage, regarding the experience as more important than the money. But she let it be known that she resented the incomes that those on our professional staff were able to generate for themselves. (The fact that they worked very, very hard for those incomes seemed not to register on her.)

Within a few weeks, it was clear that she'd transferred her resentment to me personally. Being in the powerless position typical of the young female office worker, she couldn't take any overt action against me. So she fell back on passive-aggressive behavior, the kind that women who work can get away with. For a while, at least.

For example, whenever I started another of my weekly diets, Heather would bring in rich, gooey desserts the very next day and then say, "Oh, are you on a diet?" She'd book me into a cramped middle seat on a trip to the Orient and then say, "Oh, did you want an aisle seat?" Or she'd reserve me an aisle seat, all right; the very last one, next to the toilet and then say, "Oh, did you want to be farther forward?"

Get the idea? She kept doing things that made me uncomfortable but of which she could claim ignorance: passive-aggressive behavior.

The capper came when I was to be interviewed on a TV show out of town. The station was only about an hour's ride from the closest gateway airport, so I decided to drive instead of taking a feeder flight as I normally would. I told Heather to reserve me a car.

Now let me confess something to you about my size problem. Not only am I nearly six feet tall but, before I found a diet and exercise program that worked for me, I had a weight problem to go along with my height problem. So, I've always preferred full-sized cars.

But as far as Heather was concerned, "You never told me that."

So she reserved me "a car," just as I told her to do. I wasn't as explicit as I could have been and that gave Heather an opportunity to aggravate me.

When I got to the rent-a-car counter at the airport, the clerk looked me up and down and did a double-take; I was shocked at his rudeness. I asked for the keys rather frostily, I'm afraid. He shrugged as if there had been some bonehead mistake which was none of his business. He pointed to one of those concrete barriers, about three feet high or so, that separate incoming traffic from the rest of the garage.

"The car the young lady reserved for you is over there," he said, "behind that barrier."

I looked out the window of the office but couldn't see anything except the concrete barrier itself.

"Where is it, exactly?" I asked.

"Right there," he said again. "Behind the barrier."

I looked again. Nothing.

"I still don't see it," I said.

He sounded a little irritated. "Just look behind the barrier. It's the red one. You can't miss it if you just look." So I walked outside and stood there like a fool, gaping over the top of this barrier into an empty garage.

I wasn't sure what to do. It occurred to me that maybe the car had been stolen but that the rental clerk didn't realize it. I was about to go back and tell him that he ought to call the police when he came out and stood next to me. "There it is," he said. I looked clear across the garage again. I guess the look I gave him was a little peculiar.

"It's the red one," he said in exasperation. "It's right there, like I said, behind the barricade. Just look down."

Sure enough, on the other side of the barricade, there was a piece of shiny red metal about the height of my knees. I walked around and saw the car Heather had reserved for me: a tiny two-seater.

"Have you got another red one for my other foot?" I asked him.

"Nope, that's the only car we have here right now," he said. No sense of humor, I guess. So, I shoehorned into the little bug and pedaled off to the TV station because it was too late to do anything else.

An hour later, I pulled up in the studio's parking lot, turned off the engine, opened the door and stepped . . .

I said, I opened the door and stepped . . .

Oh, no! I'd cramped myself into a space that would have been small for somebody even half my size, and now I couldn't move at all. And the host was expecting me any minute to do a *live* show.

I started the car again. I drove over and stopped underneath the canopy that extended out from the front door of the studio building. Through the glass doors, I could see a young woman sitting at a reception desk in the elegant lobby. Her hands were neatly folded in front of her and she had the serene sort of smile you only see on people who have nothing to do. From where I was, she looked like about a size three. She'd never understand how I came to be stuck in a car. This was going to be very embarrassing.

I looked around. There was nobody in the parking lot but me. I put a pair of sunglasses on, then looked around again, left and right, as if I were a thief. I really didn't want to have to ask for help to get out of a car but I couldn't think of anything else to do.

Size Three was still sitting cheerily behind her desk. I tooted the horn. She smiled.

I tooted again. She smiled again.

I rolled down the window and waved. She waved back.

I stuck my head out and yelled, "Hey, can you help me?" This time she smiled and waved at the same time. I was really impressed.

We spent about five minutes like that, me tooting and waving, she smiling and waving back. The security man finally came over from his guardhouse at the front entrance to see what all the tooting was about. He tried (not too successfully) to hide his amusement at my predicament when I explained, then offered to try to help me out of the car.

After about five strenuous and unsuccessful minutes, he called on his walkie-talkie that he had "a ten-two." I found out later that this was radio talk for "Officer Needs Assistance." But at the time, I thought it was code for "Fat Lady Stuck in Car."

Two more guys came to help. The original guy plus one of the new guys pulled on my left arm while the other new guy got into the car and pushed from the right. I kept imagining the host trying to explain to his audience that the scheduled guest hadn't shown up. I wondered what he'd tell them if he knew what was *really* going on with his guest in his parking lot.

A few more minutes of puffing and sweating went by. Just as I heard one of my rescuers mutter something under his breath about calling for "the Jaws of Life," I burst forth audibly from the car into a rather unceremonious sitting position on the asphalt.

The men, enfeebled by their exertions, gave a weak cheer. But it turned out to be premature because I couldn't get up. In fact, I couldn't move at all. And there were only moments left before I was to be in the studio, as I reminded my heroes.

They looked at one another worriedly and then made what they seemed to feel was the right decision. The three of them hoisted me up and we headed for the building at a run. I may have looked like a victorious coach being carried off the field but that's not the way I felt. They rushed me through the lobby, past the still smiling but now somewhat confused Size Three, and down the hall to Studio D where the announcer was just finishing the opening station break. The startled host shoved a chair under me at the very moment the guards reached the end of their strength.

The host was a pro, of course. He proceeded to interview me as though a bruised and shaken woman whom he'd never before met being dumped into his guest chair by security guards was the way every interview started out.

They tell me that I didn't make too much sense. I've never been invited back. Come to think of it, I've never been invited back to that *state* again.

As for Heather, her defense was the same as it always seemed to be: "I didn't know."

But that kind of explanation doesn't fool anybody, any more than Heather was able to fool me. A habit of subtle, obstructive behavior must not be simply *explained;* it must be *fixed.*

• *Fixing the Error* •

The error may be subtle, but the fix for it isn't. The best way for a woman to come up from the bottom layer of business life is to do what's best for the company. That's hard advice, I know, because it requires the kind of humility that our contemporary programming ridicules.

Nonetheless, to erase the error involves some submission. Please don't let them make you too proud to enter the business world in the way in which you're invited. Please don't insist that you enter on your own terms or not at all. After all, the Romans used to go around saying, "Aut Caesar, aut nihil" ("If I can't be a Caesar, I don't want to be anything at all"), and look where they are now.

Once you're in, you're on a roll. Get ahead by helping the company get ahead. Cooperate with management to the full extent of your abilities, wholeheartedly at all times. Be happy; smile a lot. Pay more attention to the company's success than to your own.

Cynics will find reason to smile at this prescription, but that's what makes them cynics. In the companies that I run and in the companies that I do business with, the women who get ahead are those who understand that "the work is more important than the worker." These are the women who *really* understand that bottom line to which we all pay lip service. These are the women who never drop that red ball labeled *profit*. I notice them. You notice them, too, if you're in charge.

What I'm recommending is a prescription that shows up in even the littlest things around an office. Take getting coffee, for instance. I know, I know—it's not part of your job description, and somebody told you it's degrading. But one thing I've noticed in *all* the European, Asian, and Middle Eastern countries where I've done business is that secretaries (the majority of whom are male in some countries) *always* offer refreshments. To them it's hospitality rather than subservience. They consider it an opportunity for cooperation rather than confrontation. They consider it to be part of their jobs.

If what I've been telling you about women who work in offices seems harsh, here's an example of how easy it is to let ego get in the way of one's road to success. It's something that happened in the building where my offices are located. But I'm willing to bet that the same thing happens in every large office building, including the one in which you work. If your building has a coffee shop, take a good look around the next time you're in there and see if I'm not right.

I'm accustomed to getting an early start on my work day. Often my partner and I have put in a couple of hours before most people even start, and then we take a break at the coffee shop in our building. There's a young woman who works in the building and who seems to occupy the same stool in that coffee shop every morning. She's always there whenever we walk in. She always drinks several cups of coffee and smokes quite a few cigarettes. She just sits there, buffing her nails and squinting from the smoke, and she's still there when we leave. I've seen her perching there so often and so long that I began to wonder whether she were a shill for the coffee shop to make it look busier than it was.

One morning I sat down next to her and introduced myself. She looked up from her nails, introduced herself and told me what company she worked for. I recognized the name. I said that I'd seen her there often.

"I sit here until it's time to go to work," she replied. "I don't start until nine."

"Then how come you're here so early every day?"

"My husband gives me a ride. He drops me off, then he goes on. He starts real early. Eight o'clock. But I don't start until nine."

"So you sit here for, let's see, over an hour every morning?"

"Yeah, it's a real bore. But I need the ride. And I don't start until nine."

I didn't really mean to get personal with a stranger, but I couldn't help it. "Do you mean your company isn't open?" I said. "The doors are locked?"

"No, you can get in now if you want. I mean, my boss is probably there if he's the one you're looking for. He's always in real early. But I don't start until nine."

"Well, you'll excuse me for sticking my nose in your business on such short acquaintance, I'm sure. But I've got to ask why you don't go upstairs and get some work done instead of hanging around the coffee shop."

"But they wouldn't pay me any more so why should I put myself out that way?"

"If you put that extra hour to use every day, that'd be about 250 working hours in a year," I told her. "Don't you think they'd notice that you're doing extra work?"

"Extra work?" she yelped. "For what they pay me, they ought to feel they got their money's worth if I just show up!"

"But maybe they'd give you a raise or a promotion."

"I don't need their old promotions! I'm going to get myself another job one of these days, a job where they'll appreciate me more."

She went back to her nails and calmed down.

"Besides," she said, "who has time to do extra work? I get a full eight hours worth every day. I'm out like a shot at five and there's no extra time because I start at—"

"Nine?" I interrupted.

She looked up, startled. "How did you know?"

• *The Future of Office Work* •

Another reason I've used examples in this chapter of women who work in an office is that something exciting is happening in the modern American office. Don't you dare miss out on it! I call it the "Golden Age for Women Who Work." It's happening now, and it's happening in offices everywhere. Here's how it's coming about.

Most entry-level office jobs will continue to be female-dominated. It's a fact of life that males simply don't apply for them, which is strange, because entry-level jobs in offices are quite good jobs. They're not like the hamburger jockey jobs at the fast food restaurants. They're clean, steady jobs that pay well above the minimum wage and provide good benefits. They're jobs like receptionist and clerk-typist, jobs with a future for somebody who plays his or her cards right.

Nonetheless, those coming into offices for the first time will continue to be female, by and large. That means that we women will come to outnumber men in the business world because our entry is so easy and so welcome. But we won't stay at the levels at which we come in; with the barriers to our advancement now prohibited by law, we can forecast that each woman will be able, for the first time, to advance to the level her God-given talents justify.

With women entering the business world so easily and with women advancing in greater numbers, we can forecast a change in business. In the near future, business will become much more of a female province than it is now, and you don't want to forfeit your chance to participate in the Golden Age because your ego kept you from getting started in the first place. The future of business is in the information-handling capacity of office jobs and, to a great extent, therefore, in the control of the women who hold them.

Don't assume that you'll automatically be in line for one of the new leadership positions, however. (That's what our friend who starts at nine assumes.) Make sure you'll be ready when your opportunity comes by making *now* "The Investment" in yourself that the next chapter describes.

CHAPTER 4

Making "The Investment"

Even though I frequently demonstrate our mistakes with stories about other women, that doesn't mean I haven't made my own share of disastrous bloopers. Once, for example, we had a client in the personnel business who had been one of our top customers for more than a year and whom I'd somehow never met. I asked Gail, the account executive who handled their business, to set up a lunch for the two of us and some of the client's top people so we could all get acquainted. She did, and I had about a week or so to get ready for it.

Let me explain what I mean by "getting ready" for lunch. I always do my homework for any kind of business meeting by learning whatever I can about the other participant's business. That's because I believe the sincerest form of recognition you can give any business person is to know his or her accomplishments. I've recommended this approach to job seekers who want to prepare to interview comfortably. I've insisted on it for my sales representatives who need to conduct smooth sales meetings. It's a technique that provides plenty of conversational material, and it's always flattering to the other person involved.

But I got a little sloppy this particular time. The company had a name something like the Chicago, Midwest and Pacific Company, and I suppose I thought that as long as I made some wholesome sounds about how vital to the economy are America's railroads, I'd be okay.

At the first opportunity during lunch, then, I commented on the necessity of moving goods by rail in a country so vast as the United States. There were some blank looks around the table, so I figured I needed to press my point harder. I remembered something I'd read recently about freight rate deregulation, and I asked my guests how they stood on the issue, politically speaking. They all stopped looking blank and began looking uncomfortable instead.

Gail, who was sitting across from me, rolled her eyes heavenward. I figured she was embarrassed at how shy and backward her clients appeared. As for those clients, they just kept glancing at one another and clearing their throats. None of them seemed prepared to help me with the conversational ball by responding to my insightful questions.

Now, there's a dreadful thing that happens to a salesperson every once in a while: she loses control of her presentation and starts to flounder. What she should do then is to stop, go back, and try to recover.

What I did, though, was to step on the accelerator a little harder. "What about Amtrak?" I asked, a little belligerently. "And what about Conrail?" The president of the Chicago, Midwest and Pacific was glaring at me by this time.

"Ms. Lewis," he asked, "how much did you bill CM&P last year?"

I told him. Naturally, I knew the amount to the penny, because I'd invested the time to find out earlier.

"And would it be your opinion," he asked, "that CM&P is a desirable client?"

"Absolutely! You're one of our best clients," I said. "I can't say how very much we value your business."

He sighed. "Then it is especially regrettable that you did not invest the time to discover that the Chicago, Midwest and Pacific Company is *not* a railroad."

I dropped a shrimp in my lap.

"In fact," he went on, "the only thing any of us knows about railroading is what trains we take to get downtown in the morning so we can run our advertising agency!"

There was a longish silence, punctuated by the thumping of my heart, which I just knew everybody could hear. Finally I said to the amused waiter who was grinning behind me, "May I have a towel, please, to wipe all this egg off my face?" Everybody sort of tittered nervously, and things got slightly less frosty. They were gracious enough to accept my apology and to let me start again.

Still, it seemed a very l–o–n–g lunch. But I will always remember well the lesson it taught me: don't expect to do business unless you've made the investment in finding out what you're doing.

• *Invest in Yourself* •

Achieving business success also requires that you make a considerable investment in *yourself,* the investment in preparing to fully exploit your talents. Achieving success in business is like following a recipe: there are the things you *need* (so many eggs, such a quantity of flour), and there are the things you *do* with them (mixing, baking, and so on). The media have given us considerable knowledge about what successful women *do* with their ingredients. As a result, we've all become quite good at dressing the way successful women do, at hanging out with a success-oriented crowd, and at presenting ourselves to the business world with a confident air. It's what contemporary programming has taught us.

A woman who doesn't first get her ingredients together, however, is like a little girl imitating her mommy by baking a "pretend" cake. And what she winds up with is just about as filling. If you want to bake a *real* success cake, start with the real ingredients: education and experience. They constitute "The Investment" you must make in yourself if you intend to get ahead in the world of work.

My first investment in my own success illustrates the point. I was in the hospital for an appendectomy that turned out to have complications. During my stay, I became friendly with my roommate, whose background was similar to mine. We were about the same age, we had the same level of education, we both had a baby at home, and we even lived in the same neighborhood. There was one big difference between us, however: she seemed to have plenty of money, and I felt myself to be nearly broke. So I was scared while she was confident. As I later found out, that's why "nothing succeeds like success"; success gives you so much confidence that you're almost assured of succeeding again at the very next thing you try.

An underwriter for an insurance company, I was commanding a good salary for those times. Still, it didn't seem like enough. My roommate was in some mysterious business called "recruiting." (I was so naive I thought she worked for the army.)

I showed such interest in her business (and her income), however, that she offered me a job when I was released. She told me there would be a great future for me in this "recruiting," that I'd eventually make a lot of money, be independent, and feel proud and secure.

And, oh, yes, my starting salary would be exactly zero!

I couldn't believe it. I'd never heard of a job where people worked for nothing ("commission only," she called it). But I had to make this experience investment in myself, so I took her up on her offer.

And worked five nights a week as a waitress in a greasy spoon.

And worked Saturday night as a waitress in a fancy restaurant downtown.

And worked Saturday during the day as a waitress in a hot dog joint in the neighborhood.

It was a blessing that I eventually became good at recruiting, because I was running out of places to waitress in. But I learned my business because I made "The Investment" in myself using the only coin I had at the time, sweat equity. It's one asset we *all* have, isn't it?

• *Winners and Wishers* •

Making that kind of sound investment in one's education and experience divides the world into two camps, the winners and the wishers. There's a big wall separating them, and the wall is labeled "Preparation." The problem is, the label is on the winners' side of the wall. The wishers haven't got a clue about what separates them from the winners. They just keep wishing.

And the wall just keeps standing.

Successful people are prepared people. The wind and waves seem always on the side of the ablest navigators. Don't try to explain it as luck, either; there's no such thing. As the old saying has it, people who have prepared "make their own luck." For example, few would deny, however they may feel about his social and theological positions, that Billy Graham is one of the most dynamic public speakers in the world. And he got that way because of thorough preparation. When he was a young preacher in Florida, green and inexperienced, he practiced his sermons by preaching to the trees in the swamps.

The best example I ever heard about how success follows preparation came from the great coach of the Green Bay Packers, Vince Lombardi. He calculated that there are about 150 plays in a professional football game. But only a half-dozen or so have any direct effect on the final score. If players knew which downs were going to be the critical ones, practices would be a lot easier; they'd only have to prepare for the crucial plays.

The problem is, said Lombardi, that nobody knows which of the 150 downs will be scoring downs. So Lombardi prepared his players to play each down as if it were one of the crucial ones. He forced them to make the investment in themselves that equipped them for their success. And, of course, "the Pack" won a lot of world championships in those days, just because they couldn't know for sure the future of a game.

There's something we know for sure about the future of work, though. We know it from John Naisbitt's *Megatrends*. We know it from Alvin Toffler's *Future Shock*. And, most convincingly of all, we know it from the personal observations of each of us. What we know for sure is that working life will more and more depend on telecommunications, computers, and other high-tech tools. That means the future of big business belongs to those who are comfortable with technology, to those I call the "techies."

Not to the English teachers, the sociologists, the art critics, or the interior designers will the future of business belong, although those professions are necessary, noble, and fun. Rather, it will be run by the techies: those who walk around our campuses with calculators in little leather holsters slung low on their hips like six-guns; those who make math even more unendurable for the rest of us because they skew the curve upward; those who actually *understand* things like VCR's and NMR machines and all the other alphabetized gizmos that keep the GNP going up. You know the type.

Join them. I know you might not like the prospect. I remember how we women shied away from technical subjects, the so-called hard sciences, when I went to school. Now, I admit it was quite a while ago, but some similarities must have persisted. If so, then women today might still prefer the "soft" sciences like sociology and psychology, just as I remember we did in my day, because our early programming bent us that way. We might feel that math isn't designed for comprehension by the female brain, as my memory indicates we felt back then.

But we don't need to rely on anything so unscientific as my memory. Current studies of the college population bear out the truth that we women continue to self-select our way out of success by avoiding the courses we need for a successful future. Those studies are why I'm stressing your need to make a technical investment in yourself. Here's what I mean: although more than half the college students of this country are women, we make up over 80 percent of the arts majors. That's a lot of English teachers we're becoming. And our society can only employ gainfully a limited number of us in that capacity, pleasant profession though it may be.

Here's an even more revealing statistic: the fastest growing form of education in our country is vocational training. That's the kind of education that prepares people to be paralegals, dental hygienists, and so forth. And the reason for the growth in that segment is the number of college graduates with liberal arts undergraduate degrees who can't find work. In fact, Roosevelt University, a respected urban college that emphasizes the practical side of education as well as the abstract side, is advertising by means of a sign on Michigan Avenue for entrants to one of its programs. It's a program designed to "retread" liberal arts majors and make them employable. Here's what it says:

Attention College Graduates!
Enroll Now to Be a Lawyer's Assistant.

And the sign has a picture next to this message, a picture of a young woman.

The audience is pretty clearly defined, isn't it? What does it tell you about what we women do with our chance to become educated? What does it tell you about this large (and excellent) university's judgment about us? How do you feel about an appeal like this? How would you feel about your daughter's spending four *years* in college and then having to go to school some more just to become a lawyer's *assistant*?

Please don't interpret these remarks as a diatribe against a liberal arts education; I'm a victim of one myself. My objection is not to an education that emphasizes the kinds of courses we women have been programmed to appreciate and that so many of us took. My objection is to an education that *excludes* the subjects you must take so you can learn to *do* something.

• *What We Need to Study* •

The educational major of choice in America today is business. That ought to tell you something about the kinds of courses that are likely to help you in the working world, whether you're a full-time college student or someone trying to improve herself by taking courses in night school.

I'm not recommending that you avoid studying those things that enrich your life. But practical, vocational, job-oriented courses can be taken in addition to, as well as instead of, the more abstract, academic types of courses that statistics show we women favor. At a minimum, you must become what is

52

called "computer literate." This phrase doesn't imply that you need to be a genius, but rather that you become familiar enough with the technology that it doesn't scare you.

If you can't bring yourself to immerse yourself fully in practical business or vocational courses, go ahead and study anthropology or comparative literature or whatever you want to. But at least take *some* business, math, typing, and general science and computer courses for your electives.

If you somehow neglected those kinds of courses when you were in school, you can pick them up at night school. Some community colleges even provide courses with titles as expressive as "Computer Literacy" for free or almost so. And who knows what other success courses you might run across there?

I never like to give untested advice, so I decided to do a little research. I wanted to find out how hard it would be to use modern educational opportunities to help you get a well-paying respectable job with a future. Now, of course, I know you could attend a fine university and then go to graduate school for the ubiquitous MBA or some other graduate degree. But I thought it would be interesting if we assumed that you had only a limited amount of both time and money to spend on your education. That's a reasonable assumption, because the only thing you have that's not limited is your own *effort*.

If you don't have a king's ransom, then, to pay for Harvard, and if you don't have four years or more to study without needing to make a living, what can you do? I visited with Chicago's outstanding Loop College to find out. If you live near a big city, there's probably a place like Loop near you. They charge a tuition that most everybody can afford. They also maintain a financial assistance office if you're not "most everybody." Further, they have a number of ways to help you find a job when you've completed your program. And best of all, they do it all in one semester to two years, tops.

These are only a few of the practical, career-oriented programs in their catalog:

• Automotive Technology. Everything from engine repair to body and fender work. Hands-on experience. A high-paying field overlooked by women because our early programming makes us want to stay clean.

• Heating, ventilation, and air conditioning technology. Another high-paying field with lots of opportunities for starting one's own business because the capital investment is modest. Overlooked by women.

• Mortuary Science. Not just embalming, but cosmetology and all other activities performed by morticians. At Loop, the advisory board for this program is composed of top morticians in the Chicago area, who regularly hire the best of the graduates. I can't think of any other business where the work is as steady, can you?

• Computer courses—miles and miles of them. They're not courses like "The History of Computers," either, but earning-oriented courses like word processing, data base usage, spread sheet programs, and computer repair and operations.

I could go on, but the programs are better described by the catalog. If you need to help yourself in the working world, get the catalog of the colleges in your area. Some colleges and programs operate by correspondence and by extension as well as face-to-face, so even if you live in Puddle Jump, Wyoming, our system makes career educational opportunity available to you. All you have to do is ask for the information at your closest two-year college.

But notice that I keep stressing the vocational or career-preparation aspect of the education that I recommend to you. In order to make a living, it's absolutely necessary that you have at least some technical education, some practical education, some vocational education, some education where you've learned how to actually *do* something.

If you happen to be in one of the few businesses where you think this kind of education will never be a factor, think again. Modern technology is invading *every* kind of job. And if it hasn't come to *your* job yet, it will.

A few days ago, a package was delivered to my office by one of the overnight airfreight companies. The driver apologized for being a bit tardy; seemed the computer in his truck was acting up. A friend's stolen car was recovered almost immediately because it registered on the computer in a police patrol car. Even my maid had to get some training in dealing with the computerized alarm system in my home.

There's no way you can escape the need to be at least marginally conversant with technology, whether you have the kind of job for which a formal education is required or not. *All* work will be influenced strongly by technology in the future, so get used to the idea now and begin taking steps to keep up. You can always get more of that first ingredient of "The Investment" that you have to make in yourself, education. As another of those old sayings of which I'm so fond says, "It's never too late."

But there's another ingredient that's equally important to your recipe for success. The only way to acquire it is gradually, as you move through life.

• *Experience: the Other Investment* •

Experience is a tricky thing. It isn't what happens to you; it's *what you make* of what happens to you. I know women who, at the age of thirty, have more real job experience than other women at the age of fifty who have the same job title. That's because some women let their work experiences wash over them and go down the drain like water in the shower. This creates a problem for such a woman when she tries to behave as if she had really let all that experience make an impact on her.

A woman may represent herself as having twenty years of experience, but an interview reveals that it's really one year of experience repeated twenty times. When that happens, and when she doesn't get the job or promotion or the loan she wanted, she comes to believe that her application was rejected for some negative reason. She may believe there's something wrong with her as a person; that's a common reaction to rejection. Or she may attribute it to sexual discrimination or some trivial mistake she made during the interview—the "I really blew it that time!" syndrome. No matter, she loses her confidence in herself.

In my experience, ambitious young women tend to grossly overestimate their own business experience. A banker friend of mine tells about a young woman who applied for a six-figure loan to start a retail business. She explained that she had "extensive experience" in retail, but it turned out that all she had really done was to stock shelves at a local clothing store while working her way through college. She didn't get the loan. She wasn't ready for it. My friend was careful to explain that.

She became irate and abusive, however, and threatened to sue the bank for sexual discrimination. The interview ended with a security guard acting as her escort.

Whether her next interview is for another loan or for a job so that she can gain some real experience, she won't be in very good shape for it, will she? Being thrown out of a downtown bank tends to depress one, I understand. And it was all so unnecessary. She actually had a good start on fulfilling her ultimate dream. She was a college graduate, and she'd taken some business courses. She'd worked to pay her own way through college, which shows a lot of initiative. She'd also done some of the "donkey" work associated with retailing which was *excellent* experience. It's commonly (and accurately) said that one of the biggest failings of women who work is our reluctance to tackle "grunt" work, to get our hands dirty.

All that prospective borrower needed was some more of the second ingredient, experience. I hope she went out and got it. It sounds as if she'll be a great success when she gets over being pouty, a habit that's not attractive even in little girls, much less in grown women.

The great thing about experience is that you can get it pretty fast. It doesn't take twenty years to be ready for a challenge. But it doesn't take zero years, either. What it does take is experiencing your work thoughtfully, taking out of every work experience only the wisdom that is in it and no more. Don't be like the cat who sits on a hot stove. She'll never again sit on a hot stove, but she'll never again sit on a *cold* one, either.

Getting burned is one of the things that's *always* involved in "paying your dues." I wish there were a short cut to paying your dues, but there isn't. When I started my international trading business, I suppose I assumed the transition wouldn't be too difficult. After all, I'd been running a business for twelve years. That's a lot of payrolls I'd learned to meet. How much different could the new business be? Business is business, right?

It's hard for me now, with the accuracy of hindsight, to believe that I could ever have been that naive. Did I stop to think whether the banks that financed the airplanes cared about my personnel experience? Was I foolish enough to think the aircraft manufacturers would give me a bye just because I had a reputation in some other line? Did I really believe the lawyers would go easy on me because I was obviously so sincere?

Well, okay, I really didn't think all that nonsense. But I behaved as if I did, blissfully jumping into a very deep pool well over my head. I made a nearly fatal error myself, I guess, acting as if success in one field assured success in another.

As the song says, "It ain't necessarily so." Just like everybody else, I had to make "The Investment" in myself, and in my case, it was an investment that would take the form of costly experience. I had to start at the bottom again, just like everybody else, and starting over meant paying my dues again (just like everybody else).

• *The "Natural Progression" to Success* •

Success never just *happens* to you. You have to *earn* your success. I call the business of earning it "The Natural Progression to Success." It's "natural" because it's the innate, God-given, unalterable way things are. It's a "progression" because it's a process rather than an event: it follows a path over time rather than happening all at once. It has only two easy-to-remember components: (1) start at the bottom, and (2) work your way up.

Starting at the bottom takes humility and courage. Working your way up takes effort and time. But current programming, through the various media, tries to corrupt this natural progression by making you think you can start at the top. The magazines and books and TV shows that influence us adult women show only successful women and avoid showing the admittedly laborious natural progression of success. That's why I give you this definition, even though it's simplistic. We need something easy to hang our hats on to remind us that success takes work, not wishes; perseverance, not petulance; time, not temper tantrums.

The successful women are the ones who have made "The Investment" in themselves to obtain the two ingredients of the success recipe, education and experience. The women who fail are those who make the fatal error of believing they can be successful without the ingredients that go into the recipe. They're the ones who believe they can find a way around paying their dues. They're the ones who believe there's such a thing as a free lunch.

Without superior education, one cannot properly be a professional-level worker. Without enough experience, one cannot properly be a management-level worker. Without the preparation of education and experience, one who has pretensions to higher levels of work can only be a gatecrasher.

I want you to be ready for all the opportunity that's coming your way in the "Golden Age of Women Who Work." I want you to have your credentials ready when you interview for that better job. I want you to be able to avoid acting like an amateur when you go to your bank for a business loan. I want you to have no excuses; if you don't have them, you won't need them.

Of course, I admit that discrimination is an important factor in a woman's not advancing—so important that there's a whole chapter devoted to it later. But bias against women in business isn't the biggest reason a woman doesn't get that promotion or that start-up loan from the bank. The biggest reason is the same as it is for men: it's not having paid one's dues; it's not being prepared; it's not having done one's homework; it's not having made "The Investment."

In other words, it's true that the playing field really *isn't* level for us women, but there's nothing you can do about it. In spite of all our advances, a woman *still* has to be twice as good as a man to do as well. Therefore, we must make a bigger investment in ourselves.

It's not fair, but it's how things are. Fortunately, we're equal to the challenge.

CHAPTER 5

Setting Reasonable
Career Goals

The full-time homemaker may be the greatest untapped reservoir of talent in the world. Take my friend Janice, for example. Her economic circumstances were such that she'd never needed to earn a living outside the home. Yet she had talent, and plenty of it. Since the time she'd been in college, she'd done volunteer work for a well-known, national philanthropic organization. Even before graduating, she'd already had several articles published in the organization's widely distributed magazine. This led to the opportunity to contribute some articles on the organization to one of the national news magazines, to a prominent newspaper, and so on.

Her name became so thoroughly associated with that of the organization she represented that she became over the years the kind of "highly placed source" the news media like to quote. She has even appeared on television when talk-show hosts have needed a spokesperson on behalf of her organization.

As I said, a lot of talent. But since she'd never worked at an actual, full-time, salary-paying job, most people didn't really appreciate her capacity.

When her son went off to college, Janice decided to start a business career, a decision in which I encouraged her. Besides me, she talked to a number of other people who are respected for their sensitivity in career planning.

Then she made a mistake. She took one of those shallow tests that get printed in the tabloid newspapers you can buy at the supermarket checkout. You know the kind of test I mean: "Is Your Husband Worthless?" or "Should You Be an Astronaut?"

"The test gave me two options," she said the next time I saw her. "Because of how high I've risen in my volunteer organization, because of the fun I've had helping to make it grow and so forth, the test said I should be 'a major executive with a Fortune 500 company.'"

"That's great," I answered. "Congratulations! So why do you look so gloomy?"

"Well, it also said that because I'm such a nurturing person, because I've always enjoyed the solitude of being a homemaker to work on my writing and so on, it said the other thing I was temperamentally suited to be was . . . uh . . . well, a shepherd."

I couldn't imagine that she was taking such silliness seriously. I suppressed a laugh as I told her, "We don't get many calls for shepherds in the Chicago area. In fact, of the 200,000 or so interviews we've conducted through Interviewing Dynamics over the years, the number of requests for shepherds has been approximately, in round numbers, about, *none*."

Janice smiled. "I know. I guess I'd better opt for the 'senior executive with a Fortune 500 company' job."

"Good choice," I agreed, smiling back at her.

I didn't think about Janice for several weeks. We were busy with a worldwide executive search for a new CEO for a NYSE-listed financial institution. Only rarely do such ultra-high level jobs get filled through "help wanted" ads. But because the budget was big and because the client's board wanted to leave no stone unturned, we bought a "blind box" ad in the *Wall Street Journal*.

The ad actually brought some promising resumes: the president of a large southern bank; a partner in a New York-based national brokerage firm; the president of a midwestern insurance company; and . . . Janice, my friend whose other option, according to that test, was to be a shepherd.

She was bright, competent, and accomplished. I'm the first to admit it. But applying for a job like *this* when she had no experience at all? I began to feel that contemporary programming in the guise of that women's magazine had gotten to Janice, making her feel that she was entitled to more than was reasonable.

I called her, and we talked. Indeed, she'd been sending her resume for top-echelon jobs and was fretting because she never got any calls to interview. I explained that she'd never had the opportunity to make an adequate investment in herself to justify a realistic hope of landing one of the very, very few super-jobs. Like almost everybody else, she'd have to start considerably below the top and make the investment in experience that would help her move up in the future.

Janice's story is unique only because she was so extreme. However, her story represents accurately the kind of inappropriately ambitious objectives that many contemporary women have been programmed to crave.

The most important word in that last paragraph is *inappropriately*. I'm not trying to discourage you from dreaming about a big, important career. On the contrary, I encourage you to dream big. Your dreams for your future success must be bigger than you are now or else they wouldn't be dreams. But they can't be so much bigger that you're not taken seriously or they'll simply remain idle dreams and will never become the kind of realistic objectives that you can make work for you.

Like all the rest of the contemporary programmers that make modern women want business success, I urge you to "go for the moon." The difference is, I also warn you to make sure you know where to get a rocket.

If your dreams of business success have been so top-heavy that you're not making the kind of progress you need, you may have a problem knowing how to set goals. You're probably not alone, either. Defining reasonable, achievable goals that work for you may be a shortcoming of modern business as a whole. Let me show you what I mean by telling you about a magazine test that makes a lot more sense than that last one.

About 7,800 of us women who work responded to a recent survey sponsored by *Working Woman* magazine. One of the important interpretations of the survey revealed what we women perceive to be the components of a satisfying job. The magazine concluded that management in general has let us down in an area of work that we feel is very important: goal setting. More than half the women in the sample rated their employers as deficient in this basic management skill. They cited misdirected effort and poor distribution of workloads as results of the inconsistency they see in corporate goals.

It made me think about the way each woman sets her own career goals. If she defines her personal career goals amateurishly and childishly, will that not create in her personal life the same kind of disorderly structure and misdirected effort that she identifies as a drawback in her company's life?

Let's consider first whether the typical woman who works sets her own career goals or whether they're set for her. A woman, programmed to be passive, sometimes declines to take an active and assertive role in defining her own career goals. That is, she finds it necessary to stand aside while management defines her "career path" by reference to an impersonal personnel manual. But this is the same management that she feels does such a poor job of setting corporate goals. Should she expect that management's authority in this area will produce thoughtful career goals for her? If we rate management poorly at the setting of corporate goals, how much confidence should we have that our personal career goals will receive superior attention?

I recognize, of course, that we women don't all have complete freedom of choice. The career goals of many women who work are determined by the economy and by personal circumstances that require them to work at what pays best without regard to whether it's fulfilling. But the point is that no woman can be satisfied with career goals that she doesn't make her own. Whether her goal is to keep doing her current job forever or to run the company someday makes no difference.

You must be the master of your career. You must set your own career goals, and that means you must think very hard about what you want. Few of us know what we want, although we're all willing to endure torment to get it.

Not knowing what we want is a big source of misery in our modern society; all the possibilities that result from our new career freedom have made us confused. But it's absolutely essential to have a clear sense of direction about your career in your own mind. You have to have a good idea of what you should expect of yourself. When I first started traveling in the Middle East, I encountered three young men who badly needed a definition of what was expected of them.

During my stay in one of the Arab countries of the Gulf, an opportunity arose to see a very important man in a different Arab country. It was early afternoon, and I needed a visa immediately. So I dashed off to the appropriate embassy, expecting, as we Americans tend to do, that things would be no more difficult than they would be at home. In my haste, I'd overlooked the fact that it's not unusual for offices in the Arab countries to close down from noon to about three because of the extreme heat of the day during those hours. Some of the workers from those offices take a leisurely meal, some take a nap in back. But they're not generally expected to be out and about.

The building where the embassy was located was several stories high, and I had no idea which floor I wanted because the building directory was in Arabic, which I couldn't read. The place seemed deserted, and I was at a loss to know how I could get some assistance. I ran back to the cab and, in desperation, pulled the swarthy, toothless driver into the building with me.

Through gestures I made him understand what I wanted, and he located the right place on the directory and pointed to it. That did no good at all, of course, since I hadn't learned Arabic in the time it took me to bring him in from the cab.

So I grabbed him and pulled him into the elevator with me. He hooted and yelled as if I were kidnapping him. Finally, he calmed down enough to press the button for what I think was the third floor, and we clanked upward.

It wasn't a pleasant ride. He was chain-smoking some vile-smelling, black, French cigarettes, and he wore a *keffiyeh* that looked as if he'd wiped off the car windows with it. The only thing dirtier than the *burnoose* he wore was the ragged suit coat he put over it. He looked and smelled thoroughly disreputable.

Clearly, he wasn't enjoying the ride any more than I was. The instant the doors opened, he jabbed the button to go back down to the first floor. But I thought I might need him again, so I pushed him out ahead of me. This turned out to be a mistake.

Naturally, being an embassy, it was guarded. Naturally, being in a friendly country, it was *not* guarded by crack troops. In fact, the guards turned out to be three young lads in baggy military uniforms who were dozing in straight chairs against the far wall when I pushed the driver out of the elevator.

They must have been light sleepers, judging from the way they instantly leaped up and pointed their M-16's at me. If there's one thing scarier than having an automatic rifle pointed at you, it's having a nervous kid on the other end of it. My driver did not disappoint me in this moment of high drama and crisis; he tried to hide behind me.

I don't know who of the five of us was most scared, but I think it was me. Because I couldn't think of anything else to do, I yelled as authoritatively as I could, "Sit!" and pointed to the three chairs against the wall. To my utter astonishment, the three boys immediately put down their weapons, sat down, and began to thank me profusely in Arabic.

The chargé d'affaires arrived then, gawked for a moment at the situation, then listened briefly to that member of the trio who looked almost old enough to shave. As soon as he understood what had happened, he solicitously escorted me to his office, where he promptly prepared my visa. My driver hunkered down against the wall outside, his eyes very big.

"I trust our guards did not disturb you," the chargé d'affaires said as he worked.

"Well, maybe a bit," I admitted. "I hope they won't take up their guns again as I leave."

"Oh, but yes!" he protested. "I'm sure the men will want to escort you to your hotel. They think you are a wonderful woman. They will want to do you an honor. They are very grateful to you. Very grateful, indeed."

I couldn't think of any reason why the lads should be grateful to me and told him so.

"They are not very experienced, those men," he answered. "This is a quiet post. Being stationed here is, as you Americans would say, 'nice work if you can get it.' They do not often need to handle their weapons, except to clean them, so they were very afraid when you suddenly stepped off the elevator. You know, nobody ever comes here at this time of day."

Oops. I mentally paraphrased what Noel Coward said: "Only mad dogs and Englishmen [and American businesswomen] go out in the noonday sun."

"They thought the embassy was under attack," he said. "They thought your man was a terrorist."

A reasonable mistake, looking back on it.

"The men are very grateful to you for telling them what to do," he concluded. "They are relieved they did not have to shoot anybody. It would have been a terrible thing to have on their consciences. You have saved them great pain. Yes, it was kind of you to direct them so firmly."

• *Taking Charge* •

Few of us need direction in our work as badly as those young men did. But we all do need *some* direction in our working lives. When a woman fails to supply her own direction, that lets someone else try to supply it for her, just as I did for those young soldiers. But a woman's goals for her career ought to be something she decides for herself.

The goals that are the subject of this chapter need not be communicated to anyone else. They are private. They are *your* agenda; they are what *you* want out of work. They can be anything you want them to be, from very grand goals to very modest ones. No one has the right to tell you that you've set your goals too high or too low. Your career goals are potentially a source of internal conflict if they're not goals you can live with. That makes them important, at least as important to each of us as management's corporate goals are to the company.

Frequently, I meet the kind of woman who insists that her goal is to dedicate herself absolutely to the company's goals, to give her all for the firm. In some circles, this kind of exaggeration of one's commitment to business is fashionable.

The truth, however, is that every woman who works does so because of what *she* gets out of work. Money is only one aspect of why we work, although a very important one. We must not overlook the fact that work fills other needs as well. For more and more of us, an aspect of our work even more important than our pay is the self-esteem we get from it.

All in all, our careers are pretty important aspects of our lives, wouldn't you agree? Not the most important aspects, maybe, but important enough that they warrant serious and thoughtful planning. That's why I urge you in this chapter to be sure your career goals are honest, which is to say achievable, and not just nebulous wishes. That is, if your career goal is "to get to the top" without any notion of the methods you'll use to get there or the steps to be visited along the way, then your goal setting has been vague and idle. It's every bit as bad as that which we women condemned in the *Working Woman* survey.

The freedom to set goals for your career implies a certain responsibility. If your personal career goals are poorly defined and you try to point your finger at management, three of your fingers will be pointing back at you; each of us who has poor career goals must look to herself. Each of us, regardless of her station in the company, is a manager—the manager of her own career. And no one can climb the career ladder safely unless she knows where the rungs are and when to step off.

It's my habit to reach for my trusty *Webster's* when writing about fundamentals like goals; the more basic a concept is, the more likely that we all have different ideas of what it means. When I looked up *goal*, I found two definitions that might be of interest to women who work. First was the dry and unadorned identity of the word: "the end toward which effort is directed."

That's clear enough. When management identifies goals, it identifies an end result to which our energies are to be directed: improved quality, increased sales, or whatever. Of course, when a goal is specified properly, words such as *improve* or *increase* should be replaced by phrases with greater precision: "produce 10 percent fewer defects" rather than "improve quality," for instance. The use of precise language allows progress toward a goal to be measured.

The idea of making *progress toward* a goal implies that reaching the goal isn't something that happens all at once, but that there are measurable steps along the way. Just so, the path to your ultimate career goal must be in measurable and achievable steps; they are the rungs on the career ladder.

There was another definition that hadn't even occurred to me, however, until I saw it in the dictionary. And yet it struck me as being a perfect description of the way many modern young women specify their career goals. A goal is also defined as "an area to be reached safely *in children's games*" (emphasis added). Characteristically, children's games involve a great deal of action and squealing and blundering about, but almost no planning and strategy. In contrast, our respect for our personal goals should be such that we define them with as much careful thought as the chess game that companies go through when setting their corporate business goals.

• *The Importance of Short-Term Goals* •

If setting our personal career goals is anything like setting our company's business goals, we should also be able to monitor them the same way. That is, we should be able to measure our progress step by step over time to be sure that we're on the right track toward achieving our desired end. The best way to insure that is to have a series of small, short-term, achievable, measurable objectives leading to your one big goal.

Unfortunately, it's been my experience that we women frequently allow our career goals to be vague. I've also found that ambitious, educated young women are the worst offenders. They often state their goals simply as, "I want to get into management" (Oh, how I hate that phrase!) or "I want to have my own company." Such statements ought to be accompanied by some sign of recognition that dues must be paid before the goal can be reached. Those dues may be in the form of education or experience or attitude, but they must always be paid. They must reflect the effort you've made to be ready for success. They must reflect "The Investment" in yourself that justifies success. But insisting on highflying goals without conscientious planning and preparation is the same behavior we see in the child who races heedlessly for the goal in "tag" without any thought of strategy or tactics, just as that second definition suggests.

Realistically, though, how could we expect the situation to be otherwise? Since earliest childhood, have we not been programmed to aspire to goals that are big and far off in terms of time? I remember hearing as a child expressions like "when you have your own home" or "when you have a family." That kind of programming statement tends to trivialize the precious time between now and the day the ultimate goal is realized. A lot of good and important things happened to me between the time I was a child and the time I grew to have my own home.

That's the case with all of us. We should avoid making only the grand and distant goals seem worthwhile to our daughters. Programming statements that cause little girls to focus on the far future instead of the wonderful time between now and then are dangerous. They get us accustomed to thinking only in terms of very big, very distant goals, and the habit carries over into our working lives. Little girls go through their childhoods dreaming of and acting out their big wedding day. They spend their adolescence leafing through bride magazines (of which there are more today than ever before, incidentally, just in case you were thinking that such programming is a thing of the past). Our contemporary programming only makes the problem worse by making us envious through all the magazine articles and TV shows of glamorous individual successes among women. It all works together to make us dreamers.

That's how it happens that we set our career goals so poorly: the fairy tales persist for many of us, and they carry over into our working lives. We still daydream about our jobs. We see the CEO or the managing partner as Prince Charming. We see ourselves being swept up to executive country some day. We see ourselves living happily ever after, just as did Cinderella or the Ugly Duckling.

Nonsense.

You're setting yourself up for failure if you don't have goals for your working life that are, above all, realistic. If you haven't made "The Investment" in yourself that equips you for upper management, don't set upper management as one of your goals. At least not until you've put the objectives of getting the appropriate education and experience and attitude in front of it. Those somewhat more easily achieved objectives may require still more easily achieved objectives (registering in night school, for example).

• *The Success Habit* •

You see how it works? You can build a "success habit" for yourself. And in order to experience success so frequently that it becomes a habit, the goals you define must be such that you can achieve them quickly. In the case of the goal to start making "The Investment" in yourself, your first objective might be getting information from your local college on management courses. Not taking the courses even. Not enrolling for them. Just getting the information.

And when you've taken time out from your life to hike over there and get the course catalog and talk to somebody in the admissions office, count that as one goal met on your way toward the faraway goal of becoming an important executive at your company. Count it as one rung made good on your career ladder.

The "success habit" is behind all good goal setting, whether your concern is for your personal career goals or for other goals such as filling your sales quota or whatever. That is, it's a habit based on experiencing success with a *series* of goals that are achievable, measurable, and short-term. That habit will inevitably lead to success with your one big goal.

To have the success habit, you must be able to measure a success, a goal met, each day. The success doesn't have to be

69

big. It just has to be something that demonstrates to yourself that you can do what you say you can do. The invigorating experience of a success is indispensable to the idea of "progress" or "movement toward" some ultimate goal.

What the success habit is all about is confidence, the most important asset of any woman who works. Confidence is so indispensable to getting ahead that entire books are devoted to its cultivation, including my previous book aimed specifically at those looking for a new job (*The Insider's Guide to Finding the Right Job,* Nashville: Thomas Nelson, 1986). But what they all come down to is developing the success habit, because it's the most obvious difference between she who is successful and she who is not. She who is successful has made a habit out of doing what others only rarely do: she has the habit of seeing herself as successful in her own mind's eye. And that perception is justified by her confidence that she will accomplish what she says she can.

Without the success habit, you run the risk of becoming a casualty of disappointment and depression. That's because without the success habit, you won't see enough progress toward a faraway goal to prevent frustration, no matter how badly you want that ultimate goal or how hard you're willing to work at it. Without the confidence you can only get from the daily experience of success, you'll have that familiar sensation of spinning your wheels. Every day that goes by will feel like another failure. And soon *failure* will become a habit.

When failure becomes a habit, you lose your confidence in yourself, and you lose the self-esteem that may be one of the biggest reasons you work. Your job becomes a hassle rather than a source of pleasure. The "failure habit" is just as harmful to your career as the success habit is helpful.

The failure habit that results from having unrealistic goals may even be one of the reasons we women drop out of the working force. The problem has reached the magnitude that *Fortune* magazine devoted a recent cover story to it. In fact, of our best and brightest, of those who should be our standard-bearers—the female MBA's—30 percent are now estimated to be dropping out of the fast-track career world they worked so hard to get into in the first place.

To be sure, there are additional reasons for this alarming mortality rate, the desire to start and raise a family foremost among them. And in those cases where motherhood is the motivation, we can applaud the behavior; homemaking is one of the many fulfilling careers we women are free to choose.

But in interviews with women who drop out, there's often a disquieting undercurrent that it's all much tougher than they thought. It's really an admission that their goals were poorly set, isn't it? It's an embarrassing admission that some of us didn't know what we were letting ourselves in for.

None of us ever fools herself for long, though. The disparity between idle wishes or fairy tales and actual progress (or lack of progress) quickly becomes apparent. A woman who's a victim of the contemporary programming that makes her insist on glittery career goals either drops out or becomes driven. One easily identifiable kind of woman produced by this career obsession is the overachiever who drives herself relentlessly until she has no time for herself or anybody else: "Wonder Woman."

• *The Wonder Woman Mentality* •

Wonder Woman is becoming more and more familiar in modern business. She seems to be especially numerous in big cities and in service industries. Perhaps that's because city women in fast-moving service businesses are exposed more often to the media's contemporary programming about the singular importance of their careers. In any event, this programming is enormously successful on Wonder Woman. She tries to do everything better than anybody else, and she actually succeeds. For a while.

She performs dazzlingly on a demanding job. She competes and wins on the corporate fast track. She arranges for "quality time" with her family so she can be the perfect wife and mother. She somehow manages to keep herself in great shape and to look terrific all the time. She's competent. She's admired. She's everything to everybody.

71

While most of us simply say, "I want it all and I want it now," for her it's a statement of her circumstances rather than of her desires. She's a high achiever.

Maybe she's an overachiever.

Her unreasonable goal to be everything to everybody sets up a dangerous internal conflict. The normal stresses associated with a high-level career, with raising a family, and with modern life in general put big demands on everybody. But in Wonder Woman they accumulate to an overstressed level of pressure where "something's gotta give."

Psychologist Harriet Braiker has described Wonder Woman as suffering from "Type E Stress." Dr. Braiker describes the syndrome in her book *The Type E Woman—How to Overcome the Stress of Being Everything to Everyone.* Her definition corresponds well to another of the stereotypes about us, the one that asks you to accept that we women really *are* different. She makes the point that women manifest stress differently from the way men do. Where men openly express stress as anger and frustration, women are much more likely to direct stress inward, to experience it as guilt or as a feeling of inadequacy. That's because we women, programmed to be the caretakers of other people's lives, are conditioned to prefer harmony and happiness in our relationships. We internalize negative emotions and overstress ourselves with their burden.

Many of us try to deny the stereotypes about us women that result in these psychological differences. But subconsciously, everybody knows they exist. When a man expresses his frustration in a business setting, he's acknowledged to have "lost his temper," a bad thing to do. But a woman expressing the same feelings and acting exactly the same way is said to be "hysterical," a far worse accusation. Indeed, *hysterical* is another one of those loaded words; it comes from the Greek *hysterikos,* which means "womb," and reflects the idea that uncontrollable emotion is characteristically female and is an inevitable result of biology.

So Wonder Woman is goaded by contemporary programming into pushing herself relentlessly to fulfill demanding career goals. But early programming hasn't prepared her for the conflict (and sometimes even the hostility) that accompanies such striving. And biology requires her to respond to her family's multitude of needs. Yet she doesn't dare display the frustrations, disappointments, and dissatisfactions that accompany all this juggling. The situation is enormously stressful, and Wonder Woman can sometimes be eaten alive by it.

Just like the overreaching pilot who "pushes the limits of the envelope," there's a good chance Wonder Woman will crash and burn.

Being Wonder Woman is a problem to be solved, not the source of pride that contemporary programming tries to convince us it is. Being Wonder Woman only leads to the same kind of trouble that other obsessions lead to. I should know, because I'm a recovering E-type woman myself.

Trying to raise two boys to manhood, while simultaneously running two businesses, made for a situation where something had to give. In my case, it was my relationship with my husband, who got tired of seeing me off at airports and never having a wife at home. He used words like *emasculation* to try to make me see how my driven lifestyle made him feel. But Wonder Woman couldn't hear anything at that time unless it related to her own success.

Looking back on it, I can see that overwork is like any other addiction; one can never be completely "cured" but only "recovering." That's why I describe myself as a recovering E-type woman. I keep my goals reasonable today, but it requires constant vigilance, and that's difficult.

It does, on the other hand, help me appreciate what I have. My older son, Bill, is grown and has a family of his own. He's a pillar of his community and a blessing to me. My younger, Dwight, will also be a successful and upstanding man someday—unless they hang him first. But both my boys are lights in my life, and I know that it's only through the grace of God that they've both turned out so very well.

Now I've got my priorities ordered. My faith and my family come first. Then my businesses and my employees. Then all the other things.

You may have noticed that there was no mention of a husband in that list of priorities. I can't accommodate one. It's the price I've had to pay. That's because after losing my husband, I made the decision to place my career above hopes of marrying again. Had I not made that decision, could my life have been different? *Should* it have been different? Perhaps so; I have my share of regrets. But it's the choice I made, and nothing has happened to change it since I made it.

I've told you all this about myself for a reason: so you understand that trying to be Wonder Woman is an aberration to be avoided. There's always a price to be paid if you want to realize goals that are set imprudently high. It's such an important concern that you'll be asked in a later chapter to recalculate the price and be sure you want to pay it. But let me warn you in advance: you might decide you'd rather try to recover from this modern obsession with career success, this aberration of overreaching.

As the first step to becoming a recovering Type E like Dr. Braiker (and like me), reassess those career goals. Weigh the warning of the poet Robert Frost: "By working faithfully eight hours a day, you may eventually get to be a boss and work twelve hours a day." Let the concepts of balance and moderation into your life. Consider whether your career goals are reasonable or killers. You may come to decide that you don't really need to get all the way to the top, that the view from halfway up the ladder isn't so bad after all.

Wonder Woman gets in trouble because she tries to achieve perfection both in the workplace and in the home. She gives too much. But remember, there's one thing worse: giving too little.

So try to make your goals for your career balanced. Try to make them appropriate to the price you feel you can afford to pay. Most of all, don't take it all so seriously. It's okay to moderate your goals if you need to. You're under no moral compulsion to be the top banana in your company. It's your choice, and you need apologize to no one if you choose to set less lofty goals for yourself than all the women's magazines seem to think you should. As the great Eleanor Roosevelt said, "No one can make you feel inferior without your consent."

CHAPTER 6

Overcoming Passivity

Everybody likes to be noticed. Mark Twain wrote about how Tom Sawyer walked on his hands to impress his girlfriend, Becky. Tom drew attention to himself by being active. He probably grew up to be good at what today we in business would call "self-promotion." Becky, on the other hand, seemed to do nothing to merit all this effort except to be cute. Tom *forced* our attention, while Becky merely *invited* it. It's an example of the way we women have learned to compete: by being chosen rather than by doing the choosing. Of course, we also run the same risk as Becky. Everybody remembers Tom Sawyer, but who remembers her?

On the other hand, I tried to emulate Tom after reading the book and almost broke my neck; maybe Becky had something there after all.

Programming hasn't really changed much since Mark Twain's day, has it? We women who work still adopt passive strategies for getting ahead. We still invite superiors to notice us rather than compelling them to do so. That is, we do our jobs well and expect that promotion will follow as a result of good work. Such a passive pursuit of promotion would be justified only in a world where promotion is a reward for doing one's job well. But in "the real world" that we all like to talk about, promotion need *not* follow as the result of doing your job well, nor should you expect it to. Doing your job well is *necessary* to getting promoted, but it isn't *sufficient*. It's only half of what's needed to ensure promotion.

If this sounds cynical, it's only because many people think that promotion is a reward for good work. But that's not what a promotion is, is it? It's a challenge. If promotion were a reward, one who was promoted would keep doing what she'd been doing well, only more of it.

• *What Is a Promotion?* •

In reality, of course, promotion is not doing more of what you've been doing but doing *something else*. And a higher level job requires different qualities and skills from those you've been displaying on your present assignment. Supervisory positions, for example, require more "people skills" than do operational positions.

So if you want to be promoted, you have to cause your boss to understand that you have the requisite talents *not only for your present job, but for the job you'd like to have as well*.

That explains a phenomenon that sometimes confuses women who work: the best worker is not automatically the one chosen for promotion. To many of us this seems unfair, but is it? Remember that promotion is *not* a reward for performance. So if the promotion goes to someone other than the best performer, why should that surprise you?

"Fairness" doesn't enter into it.

Understanding that promotion is not your reward for doing a good job explains why promotions so often go to those who are best at putting themselves forward, who are assertive, even pushy. Those characteristics may be among the traits required for that next level up.

It's good to remind you once in a while that all the remarks in this book are valid only at this time in our history and in America. But as American business becomes increasingly international, some of us will wind up working in situations where actions that are examples of desirable modern American behavior turn out to be contrary to one's interests. In fact, they can be disastrous.

Take, for example, that remark I made above about how pushiness may sometimes be a good thing to have in your personality inventory. If you work for a Japanese company, as more and more of us do, you may want to temper the amount of "pushiness" you display. Go with your programming then, because the Japanese esteem the same kind of harmony that we American women have been trained to foster. Or if you work for an Arab company, you may find the ability to smilingly endure interminable negotiations a benefit. Again, it's probably best to go with your programming, because Arabs admire the kind of intense and detailed scrutiny we women have been taught to bring to bear before we act.

In America today, though, promotion requires mental and emotional toughness. We American women can develop that toughness to deal with our American male counterparts once we know what our programming has been.

• *An Unusual Culture* •

There's another foreign power that's just now beginning to make its clout felt on the American business scene, the People's Republic of China (PRC). The more international we become in this country, the more likely it is that you will wind up working for a country that is as different from America as is the PRC.

A few years ago, I tried to move into this new market, just as did so many other American business people. It's a culture that respects neither pushness nor passivity. It's a culture that seems to prize only one characteristic in its business partners: integrity.

I was trying to sell some planes to one of the PRC's airlines. Their airlines are neither privately owned (like ours) nor federally owned (like many of Europe's). Rather, each province and each region has its own airline. In other words, try to imagine a United States in which there was no United

Airlines, no Delta, no Eastern. Instead there were a lot of airlines such as, maybe, AirArkansas, TransTennessee, and Pan-Pennsylvania. Go try to sell airplanes, right?

Anyway, we were in the third day of a meeting that was about, as near as I can now recall, what we would talk about when the *real* meetings began. A gentleman who sat immediately to my left at the conference table kept drinking all the soft drinks they put out for us. I found his behavior rude, since he kept draining the bottle that was in front of us, leaving none for me.

Needless to say, this man found it necessary to excuse himself from the room a great deal. I wasn't keeping an exact count, of course, but I'd guess he was leaving the room about every half hour or so. On his return, he'd reach immediately for the pop bottle, fill his glass, start gulping it down again, and soon he'd excuse himself once more. So it had gone for three days.

That evening at one of the lavish state dinners our Chinese hosts were kind enough to throw for us every night, I mentioned the man's strange behavior to a colleague of mine, an American who works for one of the aircraft manufacturers and who's been handling his company's China account since about the day after Nixon opened it up.

"I guess Mr. Wing takes some getting used to," he admitted. "He's been using that trick as long as I've been calling on the PRC."

"'Trick,'" I said, "what do you mean, 'trick'? I thought he was just some kind of soda pop junkie."

My friend laughed. "Near as I can tell, he hates the stuff."

"But he drinks it as if he were dying of thirst."

"Yes. And then he has an excuse to leave the room frequently."

I thought a moment. "You mean he's up to something out there?"

"Sure. His delegation monopolizes the men's room. Wing runs in there every half hour or so to tell them the latest on the negotiations. When he goes there, the rest of the delegation discuss what he told them."

"In the men's room?"

"In the men's room. And when he comes back on his next trip, they give him their instructions. Then he briefs them on the last half hour's business so they can discuss it again, and so on."

"But I thought Mr. Wing was a big shot, the man in charge. Why would they keep him on such a short leash?"

"Oh, he's not in charge. You see, the Chinese were cheated by some Western traders when they first reopened the country, and now they're kind of gun shy. They don't want to get cheated again, but they don't want to give offense by admitting they don't trust us. So now, although they go to great lengths to be unobtrusive about it, the whole committee makes every decision jointly."

"The whole committee . . . in the men's room?"

"Now you got it," he said.

How much tolerance for aggressive, pushy behavior do you think these guys had if they were prepared to go to so much trouble to coordinate with each other? But you couldn't expect them to have much tolerance for passive, helpless behavior, either; they're among the most determined people I've ever met.

I always remember that incident as a warning, a caution that the ways that work today in America are not always appropriate elsewhere. So, maybe there are places where proper behavior requires that you bide your time until promotion is bestowed on you like a royal title, as recognition for your good work.

But not here.

• *Speak Up for Yourself* •

The modern American woman, programmed to be passive as we've seen, is inclined to wait for promotion to come her way. And yet that same modern woman is insulted, and rightly so, by the corny old image of a single woman sitting around on Saturday night, waiting for the phone to ring.

It's surprising how many of those very same modern women find it natural to wait for promotion on their jobs. Both kinds of waiting for someone more powerful to help us are offensive to me as a woman, and they should be to you as well.

Actively encourage the recognition of your talents. Don't expect to be promoted just because you're the best in your department at whatever it is you do. For that, they should just give you more of the same. Rather, analyze the next job you'd like to have to determine the qualities and skills necessary to doing it well.

Then display those qualities and skills at every opportunity.

For example, it has become fashionable in most big businesses to view managers as "coaches and teachers." In fact, many modern companies have spaces reserved on managers' performance appraisal forms for rating those very qualities. No matter what business you're in, it's likely that managers who display these qualities are highly prized.

So begin to act like a coach and teacher. Help others that have the same job you have—not by doing their excess work, but by suggesting ways they can perform better. In other words, go ahead and act like a coach and a teacher, even if no one has given you that assignment officially.

This requires you to behave as if you were more important to the company than it has yet recognized. It requires that you behave as if you were at a higher level of responsibility than you are. And some women are reluctant to put themselves forward in such an assertive manner.

But isn't that kind of reluctance at the heart of the problem with us women who work? Remember that we behave on our jobs in ways that hurt our chances for success. And one of the most destructive behaviors a woman displays is passivity— waiting around for someone to reward her rather than forcing recognition that she's bigger than her job, that she has more talent and potential than her current job uses effectively.

Doesn't communicating your aspirations in a clear, unambiguous way require that you be assertive? Doesn't it require that you be "bigger than your breeches," that you "exceed your authority"? And doesn't it entail a risk that someone might object? You bet it does. But how else can you show them you've got what's needed to do the next job on the ladder?

You've got to start somewhere to be assertive. And you can do it carefully, without being greedy and grasping. What you *can't* do is go through the rest of your life being passive. The best, easiest, most congenial (and safest) way to exceed your authority on the job is to help a coworker.

Go out of your way to offer suggestions to management. Don't give frivolous suggestions about office decor or selfish suggestions about making life better somehow for *you*, but suggestions that show you're quality-conscious, customer-sensitive, or profit-motivated. The purpose is not to show how smart you are but to show that you have the qualities associated with the next level of work in your organization. Serious suggestions in any of these three areas—improving quality, getting closer to the customer, and increasing profits—are welcome in every organization.

Survival in the workplace, therefore, requires the right kind of ambition, which avoids concentrating only on you and your ultimate success. Instead, it recognizes that the way to get ahead is to make a sincere contribution to the performance of your coworkers, to the achievements of your boss, to the satisfaction of your employer's customers, and to the enrichment of the company's bottom line.

Survival in the workplace requires even more than displaying the right kind of ambition, however. It also requires something else that we women find especially difficult. Because getting ahead is a matter of "show and tell," it's essential that you *show* the talents and skills that justify your knowledge that you can perform at a higher level. But it's also essential that you *tell* management what your aspirations are. Doing it the right way requires a lot of courage, not to mention tact. It requires that you make explicit the kind of promotion that you will solicit eagerly and accept enthusiastically.

Read that last sentence again. It implies that there are certain promotions you would find less than attractive. Most of us women who work are so starved for job recognition that we consider *any* promotion to be a step up. But it's not true. Some steps that are represented to you as promotions are really nails in the coffin of your career. You must avoid seeking these "promotions." And you have to find the gumption to say "No, thanks" if one is offered to you.

• *"QWERTY" Work* •

Dead-end promotions are particularly common in the various office support jobs, especially in what I call "qwerty work." No, not "dirty work," "*qwerty* work. Qwerty work is keyboard work: typing, transcription, word processing, data entry, and the like. It refers to today's standard American keyboard, which is named the qwerty board after the order of the keys in the first row. The problem with qwerty work is that it tends to cast us into jobs from which management finds it difficult to let us leave. As is sometimes said, "Once a typist, always a typist."

Let's consider the dilemma by reviewing a scenario showing what might happen when you decide to vigorously move your career ahead. Suppose you started in the business world doing qwerty work because you had to start somewhere, and office support work was readily open to women. To make your move, you began to display sincere concerns for quality, for customer satisfaction, and for profit. You've been acting like a coach and a teacher to the other people doing qwerty work, even though you've not been paid to do that.

After a reasonable period of time, this behavior forced management to notice you. They decided to move you up, *not as a reward* for having done your qwerty work so well, but because management now sees that *you're more valuable to the company* in a higher position.

Mission accomplished.

But wait a minute. Let me predict what they'll offer you: "Supervisor of Qwerty Work," right? That's not the kind of job that leads to one of the top positions and top incomes. Of course, you may really want to stay in qwerty work, which is an honorable and worthwhile and necessary profession. If so, that promotion is just perfect for you; accept it with gratitude and enthusiasm. But if you really feel your gifts are most appropriate to another type of work, it's time to say "No, thanks."

That's right. There are times when it's right to decline a promotion and, for some women, this may be one of them. But certainly you can use the occasion as the opportunity to go on and describe the kind of contribution you feel you can make to the company in some *other* area.

The fact is that most support jobs in offices, while excellent jobs in many ways, are dead-end jobs in the sense that promotion to a different functional area becomes increasingly difficult the longer one stays in them. Any office support job (filing, general office, receptionist, and on and on) is a good job to be *from*. But they're all dead-end jobs for anyone who wants to get to the top.

Contrary to other jobs in business, too, the better you get at qwerty work, the more you prove yourself, the more difficult it is to convince them to move you. The paradox is that knocking yourself out to perform dazzlingly, being Wonder Woman in a support job, may actually argue *against* your getting ahead. That is, the better you get at your job and the longer you do it, the more they'll want to keep you in it and the less they'll acquiesce to your progress. You can demonstrate the truth of this paradox to yourself. Has any vice president of your company ever been a typist there? Did the president start out as a receptionist? Were the sales people moved from a keyboard, or were they hired from outside the company?

Here's why the top people so seldom started on the keyboard: I can tell you from my years in the personnel field that it's much, much easier to hire a sales trainee than it is to hire a good typist. Once they've got you in that hard-to-fill keyboard job, they'll want to keep you there.

So here's what you *must* keep in mind: having taken a support job to get into the company, your goal must be to get out of that job, *even if you have to take a step backward to do it.*

• *Get in the Mainstream* •

The principle to keep in mind is that you can't afford to be happy about a promotion in your support line of work unless you sincerely want to stay in that kind of work. Otherwise, you have to establish yourself as a star at your support job and then move as quickly as possible into the mainstream of your company's business. If it's an auto agency, get out in the showroom. If it's a sales company, get out on the street. If it's a manufacturer, get out in the shop. In other words, you need to move yourself to an area of work that uses and rewards your particular gifts and that promises appreciation for someone of your competence.

The key is to get management to let you do what your company does for a living. Take banking, for example. My bank employs many office support people, as do all banks. But banking is not *about* typing and filing, although those activities are crucial to the efficient operation of the organization. What banking is *about* is dealing with people's money. Financial jobs are, therefore, the mainstream of any bank's business. Top-level people in banks always come from the financial jobs, particularly credit, and never from the office support jobs.

Thus, what a bright and ambitious typist in a bank must do is decline a "promotion" to senior typist for a little more money and communicate her aspirations to be, say, a trainee in the Trust Department. For a little less money, if necessary. That gets her into the mainstream of her employer's business.

Office support persons, particularly secretaries, are in a perfect position to accomplish this feat of "lateral promotion" if they would but realize it. Secretaries usually know where both the success and the money can be found in a company. They usually know the important people. They usually are aware of the issues that the company feels are meaningful. With all this going for them, secretaries should be in the forefront of "promotable persons." All they need is awareness of their own worth and courage to communicate their aspirations firmly to their bosses. The problem is that management continues to think of them as "just secretaries" and to offer them senior secretary promotions instead of *real* promotions.

Make sure you communicate in the clearest (and politest!) terms to management that you want to move not only "up" but "up and out." Timing is tricky. Don't try to finesse a lateral promotion when you're first starting out on a job, of course; you haven't earned the right yet. But after you've proved yourself, after you've demonstrated your capacity for work and your desirability as an employee, it's your responsibility to help management decide how best to use your gifts. Communicate your aspirations *before* they've started to think of you as typecast in your present kind of work.

Clear, firm communication is essential, because the quieter you are about your aspirations to move ahead, the less likely you are to realize them. The more you wait to be recognized, the less likely it is to happen. Remember the old story about the squeaky wheel getting the grease? True.

• *"How Was I Supposed to Know?"* •

Another reason for firm, clear communication with management about your intentions is that management may not know (or may *pretend* not to know) of your aspirations. I learned this on the very first job I ever had, a qwerty job that I intended to help me get through school.

I typed names and addresses and other personal data on little white cards for an insurance company. I never did find out what they were for. There were a large number of us card-typists jammed into a hot, noisy room downtown, and each of us had a quota of a certain number of cards to type each day. As I recall, there were five or six categories of typist, and as a typist got more cards done, she would be "promoted" from, say, category 3 to category 2 and get a dime an hour more. She also had her quota of cards raised by about two dozen a day. It goes without saying that I started as a humble category 6, even though I knew that wasn't the right category for a woman of my typing ability.

But they didn't have anything lower.

Most of the workers there knew the system cold. They would type like crazy to get their quota done so they could take leisurely shopping lunches or go home a few minutes earlier. Most seemed to feel that the small additional pay that

85

accompanied promotion didn't justify committing themselves to a heavier quota forever. Meanwhile, I was running in place as fast as I could just to keep up.

For the first several weeks, I lost weight because I never had time for lunch or coffee breaks. I just barely made my quota, and sweet, old Mr. Novatny, the supervisor of us typists, used to shake his head with genuine sorrow every Friday when he handed me my pay envelope. He quickly despaired of my ever being more than a category 6. That was too bad, because I really needed more money for school, and I wanted to be favorably noticed.

It happened that I'd gotten the job a few weeks before summer break at school, and I was able to use the timing to my advantage. As soon as break started, I would sneak back to what we typists called "the boiler room" after 5 o'clock and take a handful of cards from Mr. Novatny's desk. I'd type for a few hours every night so that at the end of the week, I'd have more completed cards than anyone else in my category. Surely, I thought, this would bring me a good promotion and pay raise and would help me get through school in style.

At the end of my first week of self-imposed extra work, I told Mr. Novatny that I wanted, needed, and deserved a promotion. He smiled and promoted me to category 5. Of course, the new quota meant more cards to type, and I had to work more hours to again be a star.

After a few weeks of increased production, I again asked Mr. Novatny to consider promoting me. A few days later, he moved me to category 4 with a bigger smile than the week before. But I had to cancel social dates to exceed my quota, which was now becoming burdensome. The next time I asked him for a promotion, he actually grinned like the cheshire cat. He promoted me to category 3 and reminded me of the new and bigger quota to which I'd just committed myself.

It was at about this point that I began to think I was doing things the wrong way. I mean, I kept getting "promoted" with astounding speed, but I really wasn't any better off. In fact, my working life seemed to get further from what I wanted it to be with every promotion. So I had a meeting with myself and decided to confront Mr. Novatny.

"I've decided," I told him, "that I don't really want to be promoted to category 3."

He beamed. "Ah, I love to see ambition. I'm sure you'll soon be ready to become a category 2, and I'll be personally happy to. . . ."

"Becoming a category 2 wasn't exactly what I had in mind," I interrupted.

He tried to look stern. "There're only two category 1 typists in my department. You have to have some patience if you want that job."

"What I really had in mind was becoming an underwriter," I said. "And I would much rather move to that job, if it's okay with you."

He looked stunned. "Diane, junior underwriters are a dime a dozen. Why would you want to take a step backward?"

"Backward? You mean junior underwriters make less than me?"

"Oh, sure. Of course, they can make a lot of money with a little experience. *If* they're good. But they start out at the same pay you did when you first came here."

"But it wouldn't be a step backward, Mr. Novatny, if you'd let me be an underwriter earlier. Why didn't you keep me in mind every time I talked to you?"

"Because I thought you wanted a promotion," he said. "That means a higher category. What you're talking about would have been a 'lateral move.' I never knew that's what you wanted. I thought you were happy with your typewriter."

He looked so sad and abandoned that I almost withdrew my request. Almost.

Mr. Novatny was sincere. Not all bosses are. But it's surprising how many of them try the same dodge: "How was I supposed to know you wanted to do something else?"

It emphasizes that career progress must be solicited and planned. It often requires a transfer to another track rather than a promotion in one's assigned functional area. A typist who wants to move to sales, for example, must lobby for that change, because it won't happen automatically.

Remember, promotion is not a reward. Therefore, to get a promotion that serves your interests as well as those of your employer, you must speak up for yourself without becoming petulant or strident. It makes no difference whether your boss is secretly biased and won't help you move, or whether, like Mr. Novatny, he suffers from tunnel vision that obscures his comprehension that you want to take more responsibility. Either way, you're stuck in keyboards unless *you* take the initiative to change things.

Choosing to move to another track is the kind of big decision with which we women must become more comfortable. On some rare occasions, it may even require taking a pay cut (gulp). Tough decisions like that are the subject of the next chapter.

CHAPTER 7

Excising Indecisiveness

My niece went looking for a new dress to wear to her junior prom. She found one that was perfect in the first place she looked. But she kept looking for one that was "better." A couple of weeks and several dozen stores later, when it was three days until the dance, she came back to the first shop. Of course, the dress was gone. The poor kid was so upset and confused that she missed the dance altogether.

• *Women Are Indecisive* •

In the personnel business, we see similarly indecisive behavior from grown women time and again. I know the assertion that we women have trouble making decisions is another stereotype, but in many, many cases, it's a *true* stereotype. As a practical matter, one of the problems recruiters face is convincing a woman to accept the job she's been offered. The response to an offer is often, "Let me think about it." (Men give this response as well, but much less frequently, in my experience.)

To demonstrate how valid we believe this stereotype to be, our recruiters are trained to help job applicants overcome this particular habit of indecisiveness. They tell a story similar to the one above about seeing a dress you like but not being able to decide to buy it. The punch line to the story is always, "Will you like the dress any better on Wednesday than you do on Monday?" Often, that question helps a candidate to understand that she *must* render a decision.

To explain why choosing is so much more difficult for us women than it is for men, I borrowed a term from a branch of mathematics. It's the branch that has to do with calculating outcomes of situations that involve conflicting interests, such as military strategy—or business, for that matter. It analyzes in terms of gains and losses among opponents, and that's why it's called "game theory."

Incidentally, searching the current catalog at the Chicago Public Library for books by women who are good at this discipline is disappointing. That's really too bad, because its defense applications have made it a popular specialty in Washington. It's also a hot topic in every graduate business school in the country because of its strategic implications for business competition.

For many of the problems that this science studies, those known as the "zero-sum games," the gains of winners are balanced by the losses of losers. So we shouldn't be surprised that women tend not to be attracted to this science. We don't want for there to be any losers. We think a good game is where the big winners win more than the little winners, but where *everybody* wins *something*.

• *"Choosing" Is Cruel* •

The need to choose between winners and losers is a dismal prospect for a woman to face. That's what makes it so difficult for us to act on our decisions; the notion of "deciding" means to some of us that life is a "zero-sum game," that as a result of our decisions, there will be created winners and losers.

The whole process of making decisions is as yet a poorly understood activity, especially in business. Recent work in the fields of mathematics and communication shows that decision making is probably the most complex of human mental activities. Maybe that's why executives who do it well are so well-paid.

There's no reason to believe that we women are any worse or any better than men at going through whatever mental processes are involved in analyzing situations. But it's obvious that we have much more trouble *acting* on our analyses. We appear indecisive because we balk at moving quickly on the basis of logical decisions. But why should it be more difficult for women than for men? Why is it that we women appear to be the ones afraid to make the tough decisions?

Once again, it starts with the reactions to life experiences pressed on us so early—what I've been calling early programming. Little boys learn how to make mistakes and not tear their own hearts out in remorse. Little girls learn just the opposite.

Little boys learn that making a mistake is not the end of the world. When little boys play baseball and one of them "boots" an easy grounder, what do the other boys on his team do? They help him understand that most mistakes are survivable. They shout "Nice try" or "Good hustle out there," and then they slap him on the rump to show him he's okay.

What are little girls primed to do when a peer makes a mess of something or other? Raise their eyebrows knowingly. Whisper about her behind her back. Glance in her direction and giggle. Little girls are taught by these actions that being wrong is the same as being foolish, and that it brings pain.

We were also taught to be submissive to authority. Being submissive was part of our programming to be the peacemakers in society. We were taught to be accommodative rather than confrontational, deferential rather than combative. As part of all that, we learned to defer decision making to others. After doing so all our lives, we become unable to take action comfortably on our own decisions.

And so, ever since Eve decided to eat that apple, we women have had good cause to fear acting on our decisions. And women in general *do* have this fear. We *do* appear indecisive to our bosses, which is a serious problem for any woman who wants to move ahead in business.

• *Indecisiveness Is Common* •

Saying that women in general fear making decisions seems to be pandering to a stereotype once again. But being reluctant to make decisions is true even of the shrewdest and most competent among us.

A dear friend who runs an extremely profitable retail operation in a well-known Chicago mall provides a good example. She deals in "high ticket" luxury items. Her expenses and her cost of goods sold are in keeping with her list prices, which means they're really high.

Some time back, we were taking some steam at the health club together and chatting about business in general. Marissa surprised me by complaining that her profits from the store were too low.

"What? Your place is famous!" I said. "I can't believe you're not bringing it in in buckets."

"I'm just not making enough considering the hours I work," she said. "Profits ought to be higher."

"But the traffic past your place is terrific. If even a fraction of all the people who stop in buy something. . . ."

"Oh, sure. My volume is up every quarter. But volume," she reminded me, "is not the same as profit. I'm just not making enough."

You won't be seeing this woman's business in bankruptcy court, believe me. Nevertheless, she went on like that for a while. I was getting steamed up, and not just because we were in the steam room.

Anyway, that's how I came to ask my bookkeeper, who's a real whiz, to take a look at her operation and see if he could improve her bottom line. He found one of her problems almost immediately.

First I should explain about discounts for quick payment. Most businesses trade with one another "on account," just as most individuals do now with credit cards. But suppliers would rather have immediate payment. So one typically finds that suppliers offer a discount from their invoice (usually 1 or 2 percent, but sometimes as high as 10 percent) if the buyer makes timely payment—say, within ten days. Over the course of time, those discounts add up to enormous amounts of money.

But to get the discount, you have to pay the bill quickly. That's what Marissa was *not* doing. She was *not* doing it so much that she forewent several hundred dollars in discounts each month. To make matters worse, most of her bills went *past* due so that she actually wound up paying interest instead of collecting a discount. My bookkeeper estimated that both these mistakes together were costing her over $1,400 every month.

Her cash flow was adequate—more than adequate—to pay all those bills immediately.

"Why are these so late?" I asked, waving a stack of payables under her nose.

"They're not late . . . yet."

"But they're not timely, either. Why haven't you paid them to get the discounts?"

"I can never decide who to pay first," she said. "So I just wait until they send me a second notice. Whatever notices come in first, I pay."

My bookkeeper defined for her a program to help her make timely payment, but it did no good. Marissa is the kind of woman who, once she makes up her mind, is full of indecision. Today, about three years later, she still pays everything late because she can't decide who to pay first.

She's still not suffering financially, either, but that's not the point. The point is that even Marissa, a widely respected businesswoman, has trouble making certain kinds of decisions. Her early programming didn't prepare her for it.

• *Decisive Action* •

We have to overcome that programming for indecision. We can't move ahead either as a group or individually until we make decisions comfortably as well as wisely. Decision making is fundamental to business. In recognition of this, Thomas J. Peters and Robert H. Waterman, Jr., in their outstanding book *In Search of Excellence,* defined one of the basic principles that drive excellent organizations as "a bias for action."

A bias for action is the kind of decisiveness that Franklin Roosevelt had in mind when he told his advisors who were despairing about moving the country out of the economic doldrums of depression, "Above all, try *something.*" In other words, their decisions didn't even have to be right. But if they made the decision often enough to just get on with it, some of the choices would bear fruit.

FDR was a model for decisiveness. He forged ahead even though he knew that some of his ideas might very well be negated by the Supreme Court. Eventually, some of his programs were indeed found to be unconstitutional. But the decision to go ahead and let himself be second-guessed by the armchair quarterbacks showed the kind of decisiveness we women must emulate.

Of course, it's natural to fear being wrong; nobody wants to be wrong. But it's deeper than that with us women who work. Because we've been programmed to favor harmony in relationships, we tend to try too hard to get everyone affected to agree with our decisions. We tend to try too hard to achieve consensus. So we indulge in "decision avoidance" behavior. That is to say, we don't make bad decisions so much as we try to maneuver circumstances in such a way that we forestall the need to make *any* decision.

The most common stalling technique is to study an issue to death. We gather data, form committees, test our ideas, and then gather the data again since our tests might have changed it. If an indecisive female executive stalls in this way long enough, the need to make a decision will be rendered obsolete by the passage of time.

But being in charge sometimes means acting without consensus. It involves, rather, acting *before* everything about a problem is known; it involves taking risk.

Paradoxically, I've always felt that this female habit was a help rather than a hindrance to me in establishing a toehold in the Middle East. Most men enter the Middle Eastern market expecting the kind of quick decisions we're accustomed to in American business. But the time needed for decisions is much longer there, and patience is most definitely a virtue.

Early on in my career there, I had a chance to bid on an order for one of the state-owned airlines. It was a very modest order by the standards that most of us think of when we think of that part of the world. But it was attractive to me and to several other companies, all of which were represented by (naturally) men.

We all received a briefing by one of the airline's executives, a relaxed, soft-spoken gentleman of the royal family. All the other contractors submitted their formal, lengthy, word-processed bids the very next day. I phoned the airline and left a message that I would appreciate more time.

Now, let me level with you. I'd like to be in a position to tell you that I outsmarted the whole pack and finessed the contract. But that wouldn't be honest. The simple truth is that I was green at the time. I thought I had a bid that would stand up, but I wasn't sure. I couldn't make the decision to bid that my male colleagues had made without batting an eye.

A week turned into two. Then three. I was locked in my hotel room, studying the problem to death, spending a fortune in long-distance calls to my research assistant stateside. I was amazed that the airline was holding open the bidding on my behalf.

Finally, after almost a month of writing and rewriting my proposal, after numerous visits to the airline's offices for more facts, after—let's be candid—a lot of stalling, I made my decision and handed in my bid.

Then I went home, drained and exhausted, not just from the work of putting in the proposal, but also from the tension of not being able to reach a decision quickly in an area where I was a rookie.

After a weekend of rest, I wrote the whole thing off. I knew they'd choose somebody else, and quickly, too. A big airline like that certainly wouldn't have the trouble I had making a decision. I went on to other things, because there's nothing like a good hunk of work to cheer you up. I even forgot about the fiasco over the next several weeks.

Naturally, I couldn't believe it when they telexed me a couple of months later that I was being awarded the contract.

Some concepts of time vary according to culture, and in the Middle East, haste is looked on with suspicion. Quite without planning, my timing coincided with theirs. I had unknowingly waited the amount of time they thought was seemly.

• *Indecisiveness and Commitment* •

I learned that you rush to judgment at your peril in the Middle East. But not here in the West; here, we place a premium on speed. Here, our inability to decide, to commit, keeps us Western women from doing our best. That, in turn, makes us feel that there's not much point to working. Some of us feel that it's our option to leave the workforce, a luxury most men don't have.

So when work becomes tedious and boring, when the going gets tough, when it looks like it's too much to be worth the trouble, many of us feel we can turn our backs on our careers without incurring any social stigma. Whether we actually do it or not, whether we would even seriously consider it or not, is not the question. The *possibility,* particularly for married women or women who live with their parents, to leave the workforce and not be found socially unfit as a result colors our behavior by the very fact that it exists as an option. It's analogous to the situation of the white reporter John Howard Griffin, who dyed his skin and pretended to be black so that he could research his excellent book *Black Like Me.* As he acted out his part, he became aware that the option to change back kept him from fully partaking of the black experience.

Just so, the ambivalence about whether to stay in the workforce is always in the backs of our minds. It leads many women to stop short of a full commitment to their careers. And it amplifies our discomfort at handling decisions, even ones so basic as whether or not to accept a job.

• *A Simple Technique* •

That leads me to a technique for decision making that I'd like to share with you. Let me confess immediately that it's simplistic. Maybe even childish. On the other hand, there's no reason to believe that we women will fail to profit from a technique just because it's simple, easily remembered, and easily applied. Often, simple tools are just what's needed to overcome our deeply embedded, destructive programming.

The theory behind this technique is that you really know what to do but that your early programming causes you to suppress your judgment, to try to defer decision making to someone else. What you need is some way to release your inhibitions to allow you to express your decision. Simple tools can accomplish this goal as well as any others. I began to teach women this technique out of necessity in my personnel business when I found it helped job applicants make the decision to accept a job that we'd been authorized to offer.

The recruiting business works in such a way that I always instructed my consultants to try to line up more than one candidate for every job. Not just because the primary candidate might turn the job down. Not just because the client might like somebody else better. Not just because—who knows?—the client might hire two instead of one. But because many applicants for office support jobs miss out on opportunities because they're unable to decide to take the job. Now if I so strongly believe what I'm saying about our inability to accept our own decisions that I trained my consultants *always* to have a backup, you can trust that the syndrome I'm describing is real.

Here's what we do to help the decision-making process: we tell a woman who's having trouble making up her mind to take a sheet of paper and make a big "T" on it, just like an accountant's "T-account." Then we tell her to write down everything in favor of the decision on one side and everything that argues against it on the other. Whichever side has the most entries when the task is done is the winner.

Now, this is what we call an empirical technique; personnel people use it because it *works* for them. The explanation of why it works is irrelevant to them. But for *you*, I'll explain that it really doesn't help anybody make a decision. Rather, it helps people have the confidence needed to put their decisions into action. It's a "placebo," you might say, like the feather that gave Dumbo the confidence to use his ability to fly.

Sure it's simplistic. But remember, *you already know how to make decisions* as well as anybody. You just need the confidence to act on those decisions. You need to be able to *believe in* those decisions. I guarantee that if you use the simple T-technique, the decision you favor will somehow come out having the most entries on its side.

Works every time.

CHAPTER 8

Developing Professionalism

There are two ways to get new business. You can "develop" it by bringing in a totally new customer, or you can "steal" it by going after your competitors' existing clients. Firms in the personnel consulting business have usually avoided the latter as a matter of professional courtesy; most of us have a "live and let live" approach to doing business.

But during the last recession, that changed. A certain minor competitor of ours was responsible. On more than a few occasions, he was reported to have called on a business immediately after one of our salespeople had just left. The pitch he made was, "Do your business with me instead of them; I'm cheaper and I'm more 'professional.'"

The first few times this happened, I wasn't inclined to think that it could be intentional, even if we are a big "name" in our market and likely to be a good target for various kinds of piracy. But as our clients reported these unwelcome visits more and more, I began to think that something sinister was going on. In fact, I called the head of the firm in question to challenge him. He laughed it off and said I was being paranoid. But even a paranoic can be followed. And in fact, that's exactly what was happening.

It seems that the man's teen-aged son was unable to find a summer job that year because of the tough economy. So the father had a brainstorm. He paid his son to follow my sales-people around and to report on who our clients and prospects were. Nobody noticed the son; he looked just like any other bicycle messenger reporting in on his walkie-talkie. If the father was free when the boy reported, he would zip right over and come in immediately after us with a lower price and with his pitch about "professionalism."

Pretty slick, eh?

Well, it was slick all right. What it was not was *professional,* the very characteristic he claimed to be selling. It was childish and even a bit ridiculous. I never found out exactly how well it worked, either, because his company did not survive the recession.

• *What Professionalism Is* •

That story illustrates two important considerations about the most overused and misused word in business today, professionalism. First, professionalism refers to your *behavior,* not just to your *image.* Second, behavior that is unprofessional almost always fails in the end to achieve good results.

Here's what I mean when I say that *professional* is a misused word. Everybody knows it's desirable to be thought of as professional, but many people don't know that it implies a heavy standard of behavioral responsibility. On the contrary, walking through the downtown business districts of some of our cities might lead you to think that *professional* refers merely to a style of fashion because of all the clothing stores that urge you to dress that way.

And, indeed, one's appearance is an important aspect of professionalism. It's one that we don't have to talk about, though; just see any of the many books that instruct you on improving your chances for success by changing the way you dress. What we need to talk about here are the other, more subtle and ultimately more important aspects of professionalism.

In other words, professionalism consists of both style and substance, and dressing for success is dealing only with the style aspect. The substance of professionalism, on the other hand, relates to one's behavior. Behavior, in turn, reflects the attitudes that underlie it. Thus, professionalism is characterized by the kind of words you don't hear enough anymore, words like *integrity, morals,* and *ethics.*

Integrity is a word I've used many times in this book, particularly when defining what businesspeople most look for in their dealings with one another. It's one characteristic that knows no cultural or gender variations; it's valued in every country on the globe, by men to the same extent as women.

• *American Business's Mirror* •

One indication of how highly we regard integrity, therefore, might be the way businesspeople from other lands rate us on this virtue. And the sad and rather embarrassing fact is that we Westerners are not trusted by foreigners. It took me years to admit it to myself because it's so mortifying. But it's true. Foreign businesspeople act as if we Americans will lie to them whenever it's to our advantage and will cheat them whenever we get the chance.

Here's how I know that's true. One of the most gratifying features of my lifestyle is the opportunity to meet so many exotic and interesting people. As you might expect, I hear a great many fascinating observations on subjects of all kinds, and I often ask my contact to repeat his or her remarks into the pocket recorder I'm in the habit of carrying wherever I go.

Here are some remarks that reflect the image foreigners have of us. I don't believe they reflect the full reality of American morals. But they do show what others think about us, and that's one good indication of what's really going on in our culture. As the old expression has it, "Where there's smoke, there's fire."

A Kuwaiti: "I cannot lie because it is forbidden to me. But if I do lie, I have a pain in my heart about it. I pay a cost to lie. But you Americans lie so easily. For you, lying is free."

An English solicitor: "We never accept American courts as the venue for disputes in international contracts. For one thing, the case probably won't come up in my lifetime. For another, your lot think an honest magistrate is one who stays bought."

Another Englishman: "Everyone knows you all carry guns and take drugs."

A Saudi banker: "Why in your country do you never say 'honesty' but always '*old-fashioned* honesty'?" (Ouch! I say that all the time, don't you?)

Now, think about those remarks along with the following quotation that typifies the attitude of so many contemporary executives: "The victor is never asked if he told the truth."

Sound familiar? Sound like the kind of attitude you've heard before around the office, about how winning isn't every-thing—it's the *only* thing?

That quotation came to us from a man who knew exactly what he was doing when it came to winning by intimidation: Adolf Hitler.

• *How We Got This Way* •

How did so many of us come to lose our sense of business ethics? How did we come to accept the idea that conniving, double-dealing, and sharp practice are acceptable in business? How did we who engage in business come to tolerate, even to admire and envy, the behavior of the Ivan Boeskys, the Robert Vescos, and the Bernard Kornfelds?

Maybe it happened because of the way we're programmed to "quibble" in business, to lie for the boss when he doesn't want to talk to someone, to "cover" when a piece of work isn't done on time, and so forth.

Maybe it happened because we all became afraid to take a firm stand on morals and behavior in the 60s. That was when each of us was encouraged to experimentally do his or her own thing. That meant you couldn't permit yourself to have nega-tive feelings about anybody else's thing because you wanted him to respect yours. So we all learned to be permissive and to keep saying, "It all depends." The fact is, of course, that it doesn't "all depend." There *are* moral absolutes, and the reason we don't see them is that we've been programmed to look the other way.

Maybe it happened because of our discovery that so many of our heroes have feet of clay. The current generation has been beat over the head with every conceivable detail of the series of "flawed presidencies" from Johnson's Viet Nam through Nixon's Watergate to Reagan's Iranscam. One of the things these scandals prove is that people are imperfect, which we should have known already. But we're usually treated to six months of denials and quibbles from advisors and spokesmen before anybody admits to a mistake.

It would be easy to go on moralizing about the differences between the style and the substance of professionalism, between integrity and falsity, between accepting responsibility and copping out. But a couple of stories might make the differences more memorable.

• *A Woman Who Had Professional Style* •

A hallmark of the true professional is accountability. But some of us are so conditioned to ducking accountability that we do it sometimes even when accountability is not an issue. In my personnel company's Atlanta office, for example, we had a "b–i–g client." Every service industry office has one b–i–g client, the one who gives you so much business that it would justify the office even if you had no other business at all.

One day, Pamela—the well-dressed, well-spoken, professional-looking vice president to whom I had entrusted our operation down there—showed up in my Chicago office unexpectedly. She told me that the b–i–g client would no longer be using our services. She had no idea who they were going to use instead of us. I told her I would call them to see what I could do, but she told me to save my breath; they'd told her the decision was irrevocable. And as for calling to find out why we were no longer going to be favored with their business, she could save me trouble there, too.

She became more and more irate while telling me what had caused the client to quit us. She said that the whole thing was her receptionist's fault and that she'd fired her. But she explained how it was also her secretary's fault and that she'd fired her, too. It was also the fault, she said, of some of the other consultants down there (whom she did not have the authority to fire).

She further blamed the post office, which delivered items late, she claimed, and the phone company, which was always messing up her lines. And the unemployment situation. And the economy. And the traffic. She went on and on, finally blaming (in effect) the whole city of Atlanta.

Almost a year later, Pamela being no longer in my employ, I personally responded to the b–i–g client's invitation to bid on their business again.

When I got to his office, the personnel V. P. greeted me as though he'd *not* single-handedly almost put my Atlanta office out of business. He chatted for a while as if nothing had happened. I was a little steamed that he should take such a cavalier attitude toward *my* cash flow.

Finally, I said, "We're happy to be asked to take a look again at your recruiting requirements. But frankly, I do think you owe it to us to comment on our loss of your custom last year."

"You're absolutely right, Diane. Thanks for bearing with us during the reorganization."

I knew about the reorganization, of course; it had been in all the papers. But what did it have to do with granting their business to someone else?

"Didn't you know that we had a hiring freeze?" he asked. "We couldn't take on any new people until just recently. And let me tell you, I've got division heads who are howling; everybody's been working overtime and doing double duty until everything was settled."

"You mean you didn't take your recruiting business elsewhere?"

"What recruiting business? We haven't been allowed to do any. Didn't I make that clear to Pamela? You know, now that I come to think of it, I don't remember that she ever asked. I hope it didn't confuse anyone."

Pamela apparently didn't understand that accountability does not make of one a martyr; it makes of one merely a human being. Human beings are permitted to make errors. Admitting an error made in earnest does not often all by itself end one's career.

But trying unsuccessfully to cover it up usually does.

Adopt the habit of holding yourself personally accountable for things that go wrong in your working life. You'll find that this habit leads you to make fewer errors, because when you stop looking for things or people to blame, you'll find you concentrate better on the problem to be solved. You'll think about "how" instead of about "who," and the professionalism of your behavior will increase accordingly.

• *A Man Who Had Professional Substance* •

An outstanding example of professionalism involves a serious mishap in which I was involved once in the Middle East. I brokered a helicopter in which the buyer was a small oil company purchasing its first aircraft and the seller was a Saudi businessman. I contracted a local pilot named Ahmed, formerly of the Royal Jordanian Air Force, to ferry the chopper to its new field.

I knew Ahmed from several past transactions, so I was surprised to see how agitated he was when he came to my suite to pick up the papers. Call me cautious, but I prefer calm pilots for my aircraft. I stopped short of handing him the keys and asked if he were ill.

"Oh no, on the contrary, I'm very well, indeed," he answered. "It's just that I am happy and excited. I am to be in Mecca in three days, right after I deliver your helicopter."

He broke into a proud grin. "By the next time you see me, I will be *hajji*."

(He was telling me that he was about to make his pilgrimage to Mecca in Saudi Arabia, which is required of all devout Muslims and which is considered to be one of the high points of one's life.)

"I'm very happy for you," I told him. "But are you sure you can squeeze in the helicopter delivery? We can always get somebody else if it's too much for you right now."

"Oh, no. No problem. Let's see. I can get a commercial flight to Jeddah, then hire a small plane to get me to Medinah, where the chopper is. Then I can fly the chopper back here in several hops, then get the commercial flight back to—"

I stopped him; it sounded like a pretty full schedule to me. "Okay," I said, "You're the doctor. If you think you can make it, go ahead."

"No problem," he repeated as he zipped all the chopper's papers I'd given him into his coveralls. "Besides, it will add to the excitement of my house story that I'll paint on my house when I get back."

"House story?" I asked. I'd seen murals painted on the sides of many houses in the area, but I never realized they had any special significance beyond decoration.

"Every *hajji* paints the story of his sacred journey on the side of his house when he gets back home," Ahmed told me. "If he took a bus, he paints a bus. If he took a train, he paints a train, and so on. Sometimes a man goes to such pains to make his way to Mecca that the side of his house gets completely covered with the mural: first a picture of him walking, then a bus, then a boat, then maybe another bus, and so forth.

"I am using your ferry fee to pay for my pilgrimage. So I consider that my *hajji* starts now. Just think of how big my mural will be when I get home!"

I again warmly congratulated him on this big event in his life and went my way, praying that he could squeeze everything in on time.

A couple of days later, I got a call from an executive of the oil company that had bought the chopper. He reminded me that it was my responsibility under our contract to fix the helicopter before he accepted it, that he would under no circumstances be held liable for the damage to the terminal building, that—

"Wait a minute, wait a minute!" I interrupted. "You know I'll be responsible for my end of any bargain. But *what in the world are you talking about?*"

It seems that, in his excitement and eagerness to be on with his pilgrimage, Ahmed had forgotten to tie off the rotor before he caught his plane west. This would have been a serious omission under any circumstances, but it proved especially so in the Gulf States, where fierce winds frequently whip across the desert at that time of year. Those winds get so strong that they can begin to rotate an unsecured rotor fast enough for a helicopter to lift off with no one in it.

Which is what happened in this case.

The chopper blew into the airport's main terminal building and did a lot of structural damage. No one was injured and there had been no fire, for which I was thankful. But it looked as though the insurance company would be pretty unhappy with the amount they—

The insurance company!

The papers were in Ahmed's coveralls! And Ahmed's coveralls were on Ahmed, who was on his way to Mecca, which was in the opposite direction!

The problem was that I'd bought insurance for only the few days the aircraft was intended to be on my balance sheet. By the time Ahmed returned, the policy would have expired.

It had begun to look like a major oops.

A few hours later, I was meeting with the insurance people in my suite, trying to convince them with notable lack of success to honor a claim without a filed application. (Ever tried to get an insurance adjuster to give you a break on a fender bender? Same thing, only more so.)

Suddenly the door flew open and bashed against the wall. A dirty, sweaty, short-of-breath, and tired-looking Ahmed strode in, just like a Jordanian Indiana Jones. He was as welcome as the cavalry because . . .

He was waving the insurance papers!

He shoved them at me and yelled, "Take! I go! Good-bye!"

We all sat there stunned as he left like the *sirocco* wind that had started all the trouble.

I learned later that Ahmed had been all the way back in Saudi Arabia when he called in and found out about the disaster. Knowing that I would need the helicopter's documentation and that there was no other way to get it to me on time, he begged a ride on an F-4 Phantom jet from an air force friend of his. He flew back several hundred miles to get the papers to me. Then they turned around and hustled all the way back again.

He made it. He went three days and nights without sleep or food to fulfill his obligation to me. He was exhausted, dirty, and hungry when he arrived in Mecca. But he told me he felt better the instant he realized he was at the holiest place in his religion and was about to undertake what he saw as one of the principal actions of his life. I'm happy to report that he had a good *hajji*.

The only problem was that he had to build another room on his house to hold the mural.

• *A "Professional" Reaction to Ahmed's Story* •

Obviously, the incident made a major impact on me when it happened, not only because of the enormous financial liability it could have meant for me personally, but also because of Ahmed's exemplary behavior. Shortly after I got back to Chicago, I attended an industry luncheon. I was seated next to a psychologist who writes about the kind of "me-first" selfishness that I believe can smother her readers' sense of ethics and professionalism. I naturally told her the story of Ahmed, since it loomed so large and was so fresh in my mind. She said his behavior sounded "compulsive." I said it sounded "responsible." She thought about the two words for a second, then dismissed the whole business. "Same thing," she said.

That psychologist epitomized the distressing contemporary attitude about ethics in our business dealings: get away with whatever you can. Such an attitude is exactly counter to the real spirit of professionalism.

Professionalism means character. And character, as Emerson reminded us, is nothing more than "virtue long continued." Start now to develop your professionalism by developing the kind of character that prizes honesty and virtuous behavior.

Why do we attribute to one woman in business while not to another the possession of "charisma," the power to make one's presence felt? What's the difference between she who wins and she who wishes? Examine every case and you'll see that there is no other answer than character, the mark of the true professional.

CHAPTER 9

Separating Friendship and Work

When I was a child, my family's dinner menu consisted of two choices: take it or leave it. Like so many people who share that kind of background about food, I eventually let my weight get out of control. Of course, I kept promising myself I'd do something about it before things went too far. I was always going to start a diet Monday. Or after the holidays, for sure (there's always a holiday coming up). You know how it is.

One day I got on a plane and sat across from a truly mountainous man. The cabin attendant had to bring him an "extender," an extra piece of belting to be used when the standard seat belt won't go around. I scared myself with the phrase "There but for the grace of God go I," and that's how I came to be a member of the health club where I now work out faithfully.

Funny places, health clubs. In general, there's nothing we pay to do there that we couldn't do for free at home. But going to the health club puts us in the mood for exercise. At least that's how it works with me. I believe it has something to do with being with others, with finding support as part of a group. This group support idea sheds light on a curious phenomenon I've observed there: men tend to come to the health club by themselves, while women almost always come in groups of two or more.

The reason women come in groups is not related to physical security, the club being a modern facility in a new and secure complex downtown. Also, the reason has nothing to do with the way some newer members feel more at ease if they bring a friend to exercise along with them (although it's true that "misery loves company"). But some of the women whose entourages I've noticed are members of long-standing, so it can't be rookie status that makes us band together so tightly. Nor is the reason based on the need to have an opponent for competitive sports; most of the women there tend to use noncompetitive apparatus such as the aerobics studio or the lap pool.

The reason, once again, involves the notion that we women are programmed to be different. We are programmed to be nurturing, to be caring and sharing. We are programmed, in other words, *to need other people.*

• *People Who Need People* •

The fact is, we women are not good at being alone.

I started with examples from the health club because such examples are not "loaded"; they're not likely to offend anyone. But, in fact, the identical behavior surfaces in the workplace and for the identical reason: we women have been programmed to need others.

We need other people around us. We adapt poorly to being alone. And so we form attachments in the workplace, whether the workplace is an office, a shop, a factory, or a farm. When we go to the health club, we bring a friend. When we go shopping, we drag somebody else along. And when we go to work, we search out other women with whom we can share. In fact, as I know from the personnel business, finding friends at work is often one of the highest priorities of a young woman who is considering a new job.

Men do not have the same need for personal attachments. Men can exercise, shop, and work alone more easily than we can because they've not been programmed with the same intensity of caring and sharing as we have been.

111

With us women, the need for companionship, the need to form attachments, grows almost compulsive. In fact, a big part of nearly every woman's own self-worth is being thought well of by others. It causes the good opinion of others to be more important to us than might seem justifiable. We tend to have a strong need, in other words, to be thought of as "nice."

We need to be liked more than men do. That's because we women put human needs and values above all, as we have been programmed to do. But surviving in business at any level requires discipline and strength. Our psychological need for attachments clearly conflicts with our working need for independence.

• *Gossip: A Female Vice* •

Our programming also causes us to need to share information and viewpoints with other women and to seek their support. That's a nice way of saying that we women, true to another stereotype, have an alarming tendency to *gossip*. You know what gossip is, of course; gossip is what no one claims to like, but everybody enjoys.

We gossip about our bosses. We gossip about our co-workers. We gossip about the company. And, worst of all, we gossip about ourselves. There seems to be nothing that some of us won't discuss with others at the office. It's the "soap opera syndrome," every woman's "Dallas," and do we ever love it!

Gossiping is costly to your career, however. It identifies you as somebody who can't be trusted with a confidence. To the great detriment of your professional image, that identification is clear and permanent. A reputation as a gossiper marks you as indelibly as Cain.

Identifying yourself that way is a disaster for you because discretion is a characteristic that an employer has a right to expect of every employee, from entry level to the top. Once you're marked as a blabbermouth, your chances for promotion may be at an end. And because your boss has probably learned the value of keeping *her* mouth shut, you might never even find out what happened to your career.

112

If gossiping about others is immoral, indiscreet, and dangerous, gossiping about *yourself* is all of the above and foolish as well. We "tell all" because we've been accustomed since childhood to have a best friend with whom we learn to share emotional matters. Men don't have best friends in the same way we do.

That is, your husband may know other men with whom he can play golf or watch the football game or go bowling. But he's likely to consider it unmanly to share emotional confidences. In fact, intimate communication is the surest way to break up a friendship between men; they simply have no tolerance for it. It's one of the reasons that men are the way they are.

You, however, blithely and recklessly share with your best friend feelings that men don't admit even in the isolation of their own minds. And when you tell the private details of your life to your best friend, when you let her in on attitudes and reactions and impressions of yours that are none of her business, you give her a hostage. When you get promoted, or when you get a big raise or a bonus, your best friend may feel slighted and resentful. Then all of a sudden, she may not be your best friend anymore. You may find that all those details you shared with her become public knowledge.

I know you're thinking that she's your best friend and would never do anything like that to you. But why take the chance? Why put temptation in anybody else's path? Don't gossip about yourself.

So let's see: sometimes you're one of the gossipers and somebody else is the subject. And sometimes you're one of the gossipers and *you're* the subject. That leaves the times when you're not one of the gossipers and—hmm.

• *When the Talk Is about* You •

That's right. Some of the juiciest sessions take place when you're *not* one of the active participants. That's because *you* can be the subject of the gossip and rumors enjoyed by others,

113

even if there's no substance to them. Few gossipers in my experience regard truth as a criterion for deciding whether to spread a rumor. We women may not be foolish enough to believe everything we hear, but that doesn't stop us from repeating it. In fact, unfounded rumors are often deliberately circulated by the envious as a way to combat overachievers. There's really no way to ensure against being the victim of such maneuvers.

But your chances are much better if you stay above the fray, if you have the reputation of being someone who can mind her own business. Be cautious in conversation; hold back the way men do. I would never advise you to lie to your friends, but I do urge you to turn aside idle questions that invade your privacy. In other words, you're far less likely to be the object of gossip if you're not a ready participant in gossipy discussions.

This doesn't mean that you should withhold yourself from people and be a hermit. We all need to work with and through people. Withdrawing into yourself would be counterproductive, not to mention unpleasant. Sharing with other people and being with them is one of the great blessings of life. Besides, the best thing you can do when you have a problem that affects your emotions is to share it with somebody.

The key, however, is never to let that somebody be somebody with whom you work. The answer is to keep your private life out of the office. Remember that you're at work, not on the "Phil Donahue Show."

Develop friends outside the company with whom you can discuss your problems. Let your circle of friends include people from church and civic groups, social organizations, and so forth in addition to those from work. You'll find it easier to share your secrets with the right friends if you have more friends from whom to choose. Or share your secrets with your cat, if you want to. The main thing is, learn to keep your own counsel around the office.

• What Do Your Friends Cost You? •

There's a cost to *any* office friendship. To a considerable extent, you'll be evaluated in the context of your associations;

that is, you'll be typecast according to your friendships. To be blunt, if you associate with typists, you'll be thought of as a typist. That's fine if a typist is what you want to be. But if your aspirations include management, you might want to reconsider.

Please don't think that I expect you to choose your friends based on whether they can be helpful to your career. Your office friends are not expendable. But neither are they justification for altering your own career plans.

Remember, I'm not telling you what to do, I'm telling you what to *stop* doing. So hang out with anybody you choose. But stop assuming that office friendships have no bearing on your career track, because they do. If you associate, for example, with the "girls" from the office, then a "girl" is how people will think of you. That kind of language helps perpetuate the stereotype that some women are children: "Have your girl call my girl," or "Give it to the new girl in the Claims Department." Some women, by consistently referring to themselves and their coworkers as "girls," give the impression that the system is acceptable and inoffensive. Don't be misled by them.

One thing is sure: "girls" do not get to do women's jobs. So if you want to stop being given girls' work, stop letting yourself be identified as a girl. Stop associating exclusively with those who don't seem to mind being thought of that way.

When the time comes for that promotion, you may find yourself leaving your friends behind anyway. That won't happen because of any arrogance or snobbishness on your part. Rather, you'll begin to notice a difference in your friends' reactions to you. You'll sense that they're no longer comfortable around you. They'll behave as if you've done something wrong, something offensive. You'll sense that you're being thought of as one of "them" rather than one of "us."

When I finally got my first real promotion in the insurance business, I learned the truth about how fickle are office friendships. One of the things that was important at that company was the bowling league. In fact, there were a number of older employees who were said to work there for no reason other than participation in the company bowling league.

When I first started there, I wanted to be accepted and to have friends at the office. In other words, I was no different from any other woman in regard to the need to be with others and to be well thought of. I quickly realized how important bowling was in this particular corporate culture and immediately signed up. They put me on an all-woman team called the Lofters. I should explain that "lofting" is the term for dropping the ball with an audible thud rather than setting it down noiselessly and skillfully. Lofting is a habit of the weak and clumsy. It is not a name I would have chosen.

Nonetheless, I bowled with the Lofters. I bowled every Monday night. I bowled every Thursday night. I bowled practice every Saturday afternoon. The thing is, I never let on how I really felt about bowling. Just for the record, I found it slow, boring, time-consuming, and, worst of all, bad for my nails. As for the stupid shirts they make you wear—well, I think you get the idea that bowling was *not* my favorite pastime.

But I became friends with "the girls," as we referred to ourselves, on my team, and "the girls" on all the other teams as well. In fact, one of them, Christine, asked me to stand up for her wedding.

Then I got promoted to underwriter. Immediately, "the girls" began to act cold toward me. For example, one of the things we always used to do when we were together was gripe about the company, although there was seldom anything to really complain about. Suddenly, though, "the girls" stopped griping around me. This was an improvement, to my way of thinking. But it was still a noticeable difference from the way they'd treated me previously.

The coldness got more pronounced as time went on. Within a few weeks, it developed to the point that none of them spoke to me unless I spoke first. Eventually, Christine, my "best friend" among "the girls," said she'd reconsidered and didn't think it was right for her to impose on a "higher-up" to be in her wedding party.

And that's how office friendships really are, for the most part. Be honest about it: the only reason you're so close to "the girls at the office" is that you all work in the same place. That's really not much to base a relationship on, is it?

Put your friendships at work into a proper perspective. Stop letting them count for too much in your life, as so many of us women tend to do. Friendships on the job tend not to be enduring relationships anyway: a change in your work circumstance almost always produces a change in your work friendships.

I think we all recognize this fact, even though we're not always conscious of it. After all, who wouldn't dread the emotional pain of having to separate herself from her old friends who no longer want her around? In fact, some women dread it so much that they subconsciously lessen their chances for advancement; it's more important for them to be thought of as "nice" than to be thought of as competent. This pretty much ensures that they will continue to be thought of as "one of the girls." It is only respect for your competence that guarantees your recognition as a grown woman.

You know the popular expression, often said with a kind of pseudo-macho intonation, "I'd rather be respected than liked"? No good. The goal for us women must be that we're both respected *and* liked. We cannot afford to be either respected or liked alone. To date, most of us women have put a premium on being liked at the expense of being respected. But it's just another of the things we women who work must beware of.

And that's why we need the next chapter to help us deal with the most troublesome and most lethal of all personal relationships on the job: romance.

CHAPTER 10

Avoiding Romance at Work

This could easily be the shortest chapter in the book. That's because everything a woman should know about becoming romantically involved with men at work can be summed up in one word: don't.

Yet that simple advice, correct though it may be, must be inadequate, because we women who work commit again and again the fatal error of letting our love lives get mixed up with our working lives.

Maybe it's because the modern working woman has the chance to meet so many interesting men in the business world. Inside her organization she meets interesting male bosses, peers, and subordinates. Outside her organization she meets interesting male colleagues, clients, and suppliers. Needless to say, romantic involvement with any of these can easily be ruinous to her career. The temptation arises because social and professional relationships with these same interesting men are not only permitted but often even encouraged.

That's one of the times romance makes trouble for us women on the job: when we're not the victims, but the enthusiastic receivers—maybe even the initiators—of advances. The other time is when we *are* the objects of unsolicited and unwelcome interest: sexual harassment. Whether you call it being seduced or propositioned, whether you say that he's "putting the moves on you" or that you're being "hit on," sexual harassment can be the bane of the working woman's existence.

A few years ago when I was devoting full time to the personnel business, I started work on a book that, regrettably, never got off the ground. But I had saved nearly three hundred taped interviews with women who were looking for new jobs. These job-related discussions ranged widely over many subjects, one of which was usually the participant's reason for wanting to find a new job. It surprised me as I listened to some of the tapes again how frequently office involvements played a part in the answer.

It occurred to me that a good way to handle this fatal error without moralizing would be to summarize some of those stories. As I'm sure you'll understand, all the names and details have been made up. Furthermore, some of the characters are composites; that is, some of these stories I've actually heard from more than one woman. Nonetheless, even though I've told you how fictional they are, you might find it amusing to keep track of how many of these stories you're *certain* are about a friend of yours that you didn't even know I knew.

• *Anna's Story: True Love (and Lots of It)* •

Anna is easy to remember, strikingly attractive, and a bit over six feet tall. That was how I happened to notice her in our waiting room one morning when I came in. I remembered having seen her before in our offices. In fact, I thought I'd seen her there several times. I introduced myself and asked her if she could spare me some time, to which she readily agreed. She told me she was there to interview with one of our consultants for an executive secretary position that we were representing at that time.

"You've been here before?" I asked.

"Yes, your company handled all the recruiting for my last company. And the one before that, too. Come to think of it, I believe this is my fourth time here."

As we chatted, I reviewed the resume she'd brought with her. It was most impressive. She'd worked for some of the top executives in town, names you'd recognize instantly from the business and society pages of the newspapers. Along with her outgoing personality and excellent communications skills that became apparent as we talked, it was easy to see why she'd had a career of such responsibility.

The problem was that she'd had so many positions, some of them lasting less than a year. Yet there was no mention of her ever having been fired or of any other problem that might have resulted in such short tenure on every one of her jobs.

Her length-of-service pattern was inconsistent with everything else about her. It indicated something was wrong. A good interviewer would know only that there was a problem; unless Anna identified the specific nature of that problem, the interviewer would have vague misgivings about her record. That kind of uneasiness on the interviewer's part might work against producing the number of offers Anna hoped to see.

I explained this concern to her. She listened politely, and then, to her credit, she considered for a few seconds rather than blurting out a response.

"I wouldn't want to ruin my chances with you," she said. "Working through your organization has become very important to me."

I assured her that nothing would be as bad as letting us remain in the dark; we were likely to imagine things much worse about her than whatever the truth was. That seemed to satisfy her about the security of her own interests.

"The other concern I have is even more important," she went on, "as it involves other people. I don't want to identify anybody else as being involved in any mistakes I might have made. But you might be able to figure out from my resume who my current boss is, and I don't want to say anything that reflects ill on him."

I reminded her that the good personnel recruiters are like doctors in terms of their impartiality. A good recruiter simply needs to be sure that she's arranging a match between applicant abilities and client needs that will be advantageous to both. To the extent that she does that, she does her job and she makes money. Everything that doesn't help the process of assuring a good "fit" should be disregarded.

She nodded crisply, reassured that she could level with me without prejudice to her candidacy for the job we were offering or to anyone else's reputation. She said that she'd been having an affair with her boss. The ease with which she opened up to me is characteristic of women's behavior, as I've indicated before. A man, I suspect, would not have talked so easily about something so personal, even to another man. But we women have been programmed to open up to each other, and Anna's prompt response to my probing was not unique.

The rest of her story, I'm sorry to have to admit, was not unique, either. She'd thought it was true love this time, of course. He was married but—of course—his wife really hated him, so he was planning to get a divorce as soon as he could figure the best way economically. He had to proceed cautiously, which he expected Anna to understand—of course—because he was a wealthy and prominent man, and his wife would ruin him if she could. Of course. As I said, nothing unique about the story.

She told me that she used to meet him in an apartment he maintained under another name in a North Side high rise.

"But if he had a secret apartment, didn't it occur to you that this was a little peculiar?" I asked. "Didn't you guess that maybe it wasn't 'true love' on his part? I mean, didn't it make you a little suspicious?"

"Well," she said uncertainly, "he *was* in the real estate business, after all," which shows another of those female traits with which we've been programmed: the willingness to accept uncritically that which we want to be true.

Her story continued to be typical. He decided after a while that he couldn't leave his wife after all. Then he let it be known in many subtle ways (and some not-so-subtle ways) that it would be better if Anna worked elsewhere. Anna's self-respect was such that she decided to look for another job, and her skills were such that she could easily find a good one. And that's how she happened to be visiting us that day.

Now, if I've told Anna's story as if I had no feeling for her, it's only because I've heard it so often before. But I really respected Anna as a skilled and competent professional. I recognized her as someone who should be well along the road to great success, someone who should be a role model for youngsters, a hero to young women. Instead of directing her energy toward her business success, however, she was using her energy to reassemble the pieces of her life and get it back on the track. I could feel for her, but I couldn't shed a tear for her. The simple fact is that she'd let herself be subjected to an old and common form of mistreatment among women who work. She'd let herself be seduced and abandoned.

Even the most heart-wrenching story loses some of its punch if it's told often enough. That's why I can tell Anna's story somewhat dispassionately; it was one that I'd heard innumerable times, with only the addition of the detail about the secret apartment to enliven it.

But then she surprised me. The question I'd asked her had been why she'd had so many jobs, and it suddenly seemed as if she had told me all about her most recent one only as a preamble to the *real* story. She then told me how her job previous to the last one had ended pretty much the same way, except that her boss on that job hadn't owned a secret condominium. He'd had to pay motel bills.

The boss before that one was single. He had his own apartment, so there was no need for sneaking around, either in secret condominiums or motels. Whereas, the boss back before him. . . .

Well, I think you get the idea.

Women do make the mistake of getting involved with their bosses. The thing that made Anna's situation unusual was that it happened to her again and again. In this, Anna probably represents better than any of the other women I'll be telling you about a fatal error of women who work. Not that as individuals we make this error over and over again; most of us only need to learn the lesson once, if at all. No, but we women *as a group* make this error again and again. It is as Santayana said: "Those who cannot remember the past are condemned to repeat it." In other words, it sometimes seems as if we fail to learn our lessons from any disaster except one that befalls us personally.

Anna's sincerity was evident. Her feelings for her boss (and, I guess, for all her previous bosses) were real. Her case is typical of what happens to so many women today. Programmed to be sensitive and loving and to be needful of the warmth of others, we act out those traits at work. Programmed to look for strength and security in our relationships, we find our bosses to be attractive. The more powerful they are, the more attractive we find them to be. To some extent, therefore, falling in love with our bosses is one of those results of our early programming.

So if you fall in love with your boss, I understand how it might have happened. If you fall in love with him, it's not entirely your fault.

If you let it go further than that, however, you've committed an error that is likely to be fatal to your career. Falling in love can be difficult to control; having an affair you *must* control.

I'm not insisting that all men at work are off-limits to you. I recognize that the workplace is one of the places we women frequently find life mates. But there's a very simple prescription that you can use if you find on the job a man whom you can love: quit.

Or let him quit. Only one of you (the one who has the best prospects there) should stay at that job. If you continue to see each other socially while you stay together professionally, you increase the risks that your social relationship will escalate. If your love does not withstand the movement of one of you to a new job, maybe that tells you something about how it might have worked out in the long run.

It's folly for both of you to stay where you are, however. And to be candid, it's often more of a folly for *you* than for *him*. The tragedy of an affair with a man at work, particularly a powerful one, is that the negative effects almost always befall the woman involved. The men, on the other hand, tend to survive nicely. That's because they get rid of us.

The one inflexible rule about an affair with your boss is this: when the affair is over, so is the job. Your career is neither protected nor sponsored by your relationship with him. On the contrary, your relationship is always a guarantee of your eventual corporate demise. Leaving you in place simply creates too many problems for him, and it's too distracting. You become like the body in a murder novel that has to be got rid of.

While the affair is going on, he may move you laterally or he may even promote you (at least on paper). But either way, you've lost control. Do you really want somebody to have that kind of power over your career and your life? Better watch out, because you cannot fall into his arms without falling into his hands.

And once you've lost control, there's no way to get it back. You'll stay out of control of your own life until *he* finally chooses to make an end of things. Then, regardless of how he has manipulated your career during the romance, he'll find a way to end it for you when the romance ends.

Getting rid of you needn't involve firing or a lot of embarrassing public disclosure, either. Bosses are very creative at finding ways to cause us to want to depart, if not from the company then from their specific area of responsibility. For example, Anna told me that her previous boss was responsible for getting her her last job. Seems he "spoke up for her," as she put it, to her last boss to convince him to hire her.

Get the picture?

• Betty's Story: Sleeping Your Way to the Top •

Anna was sincere. But since Jezebel, there has always been the woman who makes of herself a weapon, who sees herself not as prey but as predator. This is the woman who, without using her emotions as justification, cynically believes she can sleep her way to the top.

Some women think that's an outmoded concept since the advent of the woman's movement. But don't kid yourself. If anything, it's a more popular success technique today than ever before. The reason is that so many of today's younger women really are well educated and highly competent at their jobs. For such a woman, using romance as a tool is just a short cut on what she believes to be her inevitable rise to the top. She accepts as true what Shakespeare said: "Some rise by sin and some by virtue fall."

Here's a case of trying to "rise by sin." I had occasion a couple of years ago to work with a woman I'll call Betty. Talk about Wonder Woman! Betty had everything. She'd started out life as the child of well-off and indulgent parents. She was raised in sophisticated luxury in midtown Manhattan and got to spend winters in the family's "cottage" in Florida. She was privately educated as a child, sent to prep school in Switzerland, and then came back to attend an Ivy League university for her undergraduate degree.

Her resume included a brief stint as a buyer for one of the trendier Fifth Avenue boutiques, the kind where they look you over through the door before buzzing you in so you can give them all your money. She decided that wasn't right for her, so she went back to school and got her MBA from Wharton.

Finally, she took a job with a very fashionable retail chain in New York, this time on the marketing staff. Just like anybody else (or at least like anybody else with credentials like *those*), she started near the bottom in the marketing department, working on what they called "direct sales" (the catalog). The direct sales department was a good place to be *from;* it did relatively little business compared to the company's high class retail stores and was generally considered a backwater.

I've extracted this rather lengthy history from her resume for a reason; I want you to understand that Betty was really *good.* She did an outstanding job in the marketing department. She single-handedly devised strategies that took the direct sales department from morbidity to a position as one of the industry's leaders in only two years. There's no question she would have eventually made it to the top—certainly of the marketing department, and possibly of the whole corporation. She was established as a star, and she was attracting the attention of all the important people in the corporation.

Among those whose attention she attracted was the chairman of the board. His overtures to her were welcomed warmly, to say the least. Within a week of their first meeting, Betty was having an affair with him.

He wasn't much to look at, she told me. He wasn't even particularly dynamic, as men in such top positions often are. What he was, though, was a powerful advocate for her career. Betty decided to use him as a tool in her climb up the corporate ladder. She was quite blatant about it; the tender emotions played no part.

Her strategy worked. In less than a year, she was named an executive vice president and was given the impression she was being groomed for the job of CEO. She was only thirty-two and already the talk of "Fashion Avenue."

Oh, I didn't tell you how I happened to be working with Betty. There's a thing in personnel known as "outplacement." It's a service that corporations provide for their more senior-level employees whom they find it necessary to fire. I was out-placing Betty.

The boss had finally tired of her. That didn't shock her; she had assumed the affair might end some day. What did shock her was her forced departure from the company. She had be-lieved she was protected from losing her job because she was so good at it.

That's the flaw in the logic of the bright, aggressive women who use the strategy of sleeping their way to the top. Today, no matter how good you are at your job, no matter how excel-lent are your education and experience, there's another woman coming along who's every bit as good and maybe even better. The days when a woman with education and capability was unusual are long gone, lamented by none.

Betty's boss just replaced her with another bright profes-sional woman who was equally hardworking, equally compe-tent, and equally willing, and my personnel company got a fat outplacement contract.

That turned out to be a tough fee to earn, by the way, since Betty's reputation had preceded her all through the fashion industry. Many of the top corporations have an eleven-foot pole for people who, like Betty, they wouldn't touch with a ten-foot pole. In fact, the only offer we were able to get her in New York came from a little, bald, and oily man who was chomping a cigar with a mushy end while he droolingly of-fered to hire her without even an interview. She finally went out West somewhere, and I lost track of her.

Learn this from Betty's story: nobody is irreplaceable. Your relationship with the boss is no guarantee against your ulti-mate termination, no matter how good you are and no matter how sure you are that he'll be putty in your hands. He may not look too smart, but he didn't get to his position by being a chump, did he? If you try to manipulate him for the sake of your career, chances are he'll let you—while it serves *his* purposes.

• *Cindy's Story: One That Worked Out* •

Cindy was a college graduate. Most people didn't take the trouble to find that out, however, because they were so impressed with her beauty that they failed to inquire about her brains.

She had been a runner-up in a state beauty contest a few years previously. Here's what made her unique in that regard: most women who win those titles have been prepared since childhood for their competitions. They're just like professional athletes except that they prepare to compete in beauty pageants. Cindy, on the other hand, had entered casually on a dare from some friends of hers. In the beauty contest business, that's equivalent to showing up for open tryouts with the Chicago Bears and being hired as a starting linebacker for tomorrow's game.

As you can imagine, Cindy's looks brought her a lot of attention. But she told me something that I had never before known: most of that attention comes from other women. Cindy told me that many exceptionally attractive women actually have trouble getting dates with really interesting men. She said that many men are reluctant to approach the kind of women who win beauty pageants, and those who do are often arrogant and obnoxious.

Cindy worked for a very large company, one that owns and occupies a whole skyscraper in the Loop. During her three years there, she'd found great difficulty making friends, either male or female. The men seemed awed by her looks, and the women seemed offended by them, she told me. So her social contact at work was mostly limited to glances that she was aware of as she walked past coworkers: longing and sometimes leering ones from the men, resentful and sometimes hateful ones from the women.

Nonetheless, Cindy was happy in her work and had enough outside interests that she was able to meet and get to know some men whom she respected and whose company she enjoyed. For example, she had sung in her church choir since she was a child, and she was also a member of a civic organization involved with Chicago's architecture. Having these associations made her less dependent on social contact with people where she worked. That's something I'd recommend to every woman who works: have more interests in your life than your job. Not only does it enrich your life, but it might also help you meet interesting people.

Anyway, Cindy worked competently for three years and had risen to be assistant manager of one of the operational units for the company. This was just one more reason for the other women in her department to feel resentful at her presence.

One day, a man she met at a company-conducted seminar asked Cindy out to dinner. They began to see each other, and their interest in each other quickly deepened. It might have been okay. He was roughly her peer in the organization, so it didn't look like either of the "power" cases I've already told you about. Nor did they report through the same channels, which can be embarrassing. In fact, he not only worked for a different department, but he was forty floors away as well. It was almost as if they worked for two different companies.

But not quite. Too many people in the company knew them both. As for the man, he was handsome and quite competent in his own right: kind of a male version of Cindy, the way I hear it. It was inevitable that a relationship between two persons who so resembled Barbie and Ken should quickly become well known. What also became well known was that he had just recently gotten divorced. This happened before he met Cindy, but people were prepared to overlook that fact.

"Aha," the gossips said. "Homewrecker! Husbandstealer!" It wasn't long before the rumors reached Cindy's management, who said, in effect, "We don't have time here to deal with that kind of stuff." Whether the rumors were true or not tended to be less important to her boss than that somebody had carelessly thrown a monkey wrench into the well-oiled machinery of his department, and the monkey wrench had Cindy's name on it.

Her boss began to see Cindy less as a colleague and more as a child who was complicating his business. It wasn't the kind of thing over which one gets fired. But it *was* the sort of thing that limits one's future growth by lessening management's confidence. The implications for Cindy's career were clear, and she decided (wisely, I think) to start over again somewhere else.

Cindy could have profited from the old proverb that says "it's easier for a woman to defend her virtue against men than her reputation against women." That proverb seems to say something about our penchant for attachments and relationships with other women at work that we talked about earlier, doesn't it? It seems to say that if you give them a cause for rumor, those who resent your superior competence and attitude will use that rumor to get you. Women, even more than men, will use scandal to cut each other's careers off at the legs.

Unfortunately, that's what happened with Cindy. It's another lesson for every woman who works: a romantic relationship with someone you work with will almost always be found out. And when it is, it becomes a stick to beat you with in the hands of your enemies.

Cindy did the right thing in moving on. It allowed her to get to know the man in question without danger to her reputation or her career. But, perhaps equally importantly, my personnel company was able to meet her before she was at the stage of "running for her life," which might have been the case had she not taken the hint that she had outstayed her welcome. By not sticking around until she'd spread a questionable reputation all over the street, she'd preserved her flexibility and freedom of choice. In short order, we placed her with an up-and-coming company where they made her take a 30 percent salary increase.

At last, a happy ending.

• *Denise's Story: The Woman in Charge* •

The ending to Denise's story was less happy—for one of the participants, anyway.

Denise, a gifted entrepreneur, is not your typical working woman. I first met her personally in her office, although her name had been known to me (and, I suppose, almost everybody else) for years.

Merely seeing her office made the trip worthwhile. It was one of the most sumptuous rooms I've ever been in. Silk drapes framed the high-rise view, and expensive, brocaded furniture sat on luxurious carpeting. Altogether, it was the kind of room that's healthy for a visitor's humility.

And pictures. Pictures of Denise and the President. Denise and Bob Hope. Denise and Billy Graham. Denise and the Pope. And on her desk facing her, where no one else could easily see it, was one of those male beefcake calendars with the pictures of gorgeous young men.

I was discussing an outplacement contract with her. Not *for* her, you understand, but for a young man who had been for the past two years a well-paid "assistant" in the firm she owned.

Denise was quite candid with me; she explained the situation "as one woman-of-the-world to another," to use her words. She confirmed that her involvement with the young man was the sole reason for his employment, although he thought he was respected for his work and was on his way up. Sound familiar?

"He's a nice boy," Denise said. "I don't want to just put him on the street. We have an obligation to these kids, wouldn't you agree?"

She kept gazing fondly at another picture on the wall as we talked, a picture of Denise and somebody who looked a lot like John Travolta, only with shorter hair.

She finally tore her gaze away and looked back at me. "Anyway, he has to go," she said. "Oh, and see if you can make him believe he's being hired away because he's good rather than thrown away because I can't have him around here any more. It's always neater that way."

Denise's story is more than a simple role reversal. I mean, I haven't just taken a story about the way some overbearing male tycoon behaved and replaced his name with "Denise." One thing I must admit about that point of view, though: the abuse of a boss's power is no uglier when displayed by a man than it is when displayed by a woman. In that respect, Denise's story could as well have been told about a man, and it would have had the same moral: abuse of a boss's power to reward and punish in order to sexually harass a subordinate is reprehensible and dehumanizing.

What makes Denise's story so important is that it's a completely new challenge for women, so new that it couldn't have existed even a generation ago. It used to be that when a woman got involved with a man in the workplace, it was usually with a man in a position of power relative to her. It's the kind of relationship most women have in mind when they talk about "affairs" at work. In fact, a woman's becoming involved with her more-powerful male boss is kind of classic, the stuff of countless novels and movies.

But it's old stuff. Today, it's just as likely that the *woman* is the boss. For the first time, we have to begin considering the situation where the woman is the one in a position of power and she uses her position to hit on a subordinate man.

If you don't see the ethical position I pointed to a couple of paragraphs ago, if you don't understand that sexual harassment by female executives merely continues a degrading practice that men have long inflicted on women, then at least consider the practical aspects of what seducing your subordinate male employees can do to your career. There are cases pending before courts today with the unlikely name of "reverse sexual harassment." I suppose the name is intended to convey the idea that males are always assumed to be the aggressors but that these cases inexplicably find the female in that role.

My lawyer informs me that sexual harassment cases are now about equally divided between those where males are identified by the plaintiff as the aggressors and those where females are so identified. That is, we women are as likely as the men to be the initiators of harrassment, although we are far less likely to be the ones in power positions.

So does this mean that women in power are going to be tempted to be the aggressors, that they might be the ones hitting on male subordinates who will then get the chance to represent themselves as helpless and powerless, and that their companies can be sued for a lot of money?

That's what it means.

This is a brand new responsibility for women who work today. In the past, there was almost never any question of women's abusing authority because we didn't have any authority to abuse. The worst that ever happened to us for sexual misconduct on our jobs when we were subordinates was that we got fired.

But today we women have taken on far more authority, far more responsibility, and far more personal risk. Today, we're in positions of authority that we can choose to abuse. The worst that can happen to us now as a result of sexual misconduct on our jobs is that we get fired, get blackballed from our industry, and get sued for everything we've got.

The advice for powerful female executives about romance in the workplace is the same as it is for the majority of us female workers for whom abuse of power is not an issue. "Don't do it."

• Elizabeth's Story: The Dirty Old Man and the Sweet Young Thing •

Until now, we've talked about cases of romance in which both partners were willing. But equally common is the traditional case of sexual harassment in which an older (typically unpleasant) man makes unwelcome advances to a younger (typically naive) woman.

The big cases that you read about in the paper have a lot of meat to them. But for every big case, there are countless incidents of the kind we'll talk about now: seemingly trivial, unimportant, not worth making a fuss about. They don't really have to do with "sex" on the job or even with "abuse of power" on the job. Mostly they involve what I would call sexual annoyance. You've probably suffered this kind of annoyance and have tried to ignore it because it seemed so innocuous. But here's an instance of how unpleasant it can be.

Elizabeth is one of the youngsters in my study group. She's a receptionist by day and a student by night. She's only eighteen, bouncy and effervescent—one of those terminally happy cheerleader types—and "cute as a button," as the saying has it. One recent evening, Elizabeth was out of sorts during our session. She was cranky, and she found fault with every position anybody else took, yet offered none of her own.

At break time, I took her off to the side. I put my arm around her shoulders and was about to ask what the trouble was when she violently shrugged me off.

"I've been pawed quite enough for one day, thank you," she said.

I guess she saw my expression, because she instantly looked embarrassed and said, "I'm sorry. It's just that the typewriter guy, Joe, makes me so mad. He's always grabbing at me. And if it's not me, it's one of the other girls. And when he's not grabbing, he's telling what he thinks are 'jokes,' only they're not very funny. Boy, he really burns me up! He just won't let any of us alone."

"What do you do when he tells you one of his so-called jokes?" I asked her.

"Oh, you know. I just sort of smile."

"Uh-huh. And what about when he tries to touch you?"

She grimaced. "I just turn away, you know. Actually, I try not to be in his way when he's around. But it's tough, because with all the machines we have in our department, he's there a lot repairing them."

"Have you ever told him that you don't find his jokes funny and that you don't want him touching you?"

She rolled her eyes. "How could I do that? He'd only say 'Hey, whatsamatter? Can't you take a joke?'"

"So you let him get away with it?"

"Oh, I know he doesn't mean anything by it. He just flirts with all the girls. Maybe they don't mind. But he seems to come around my desk the most. Why me?"

I told her why Joe picked her as the favorite object of his attentions: he always picks the woman least likely to strike back. That's important to understand, because no matter whether you work in an office, a store, or a factory, you probably know Joe. Often, he's an outsider, not a part of your company or your department. He may be a delivery man, a repair man, an installer, or any of a dozen other occupations. He comes into contact with lots of women on a semi-anonymous basis. He considers himself the life of the party and has deluded himself into believing that you'd be wounded if he didn't permit you to be the object of his annoying attentions. He likes to call every woman "Sweetheart" while sitting on the edge of her desk and telling her off-color jokes and being generally obnoxious.

But why take up your time talking about Joe? Sure he's a pain. But he's harmless enough, isn't he?

The U.S. court system doesn't think so. In fact, in sexual harassment cases brought by women plaintiffs, a man's best defense is that the woman invited his advances. One way to establish this is to show that the woman plaintiff was receptive to off-color stories, to casual flirtation, and so forth. Or, to use the language of the court, to show that the woman permitted "an environment conducive to sexual advances." You and I and all women who work bear the responsibility for letting guys like Joe establish that kind of environment.

To make it worse, we can't even justify ourselves by saying we particularly like Joe or his behavior. He's usually the kind of man you wouldn't look at twice, isn't he? The reason we let him continue to be so unpleasant is our fear that he'll turn the tables, just as Elizabeth understood, and that he'll respond with an injured air, "Hey! It's all in fun! I'm just kidding around!"

But let's be candid with each other. This guy is a creep. He's not as dangerous as the boss who hits on you with all his power of office. But he's not as harmless as he pretends, either. We're not talking about romance in this case. We're talking about a disgusting habit some men have that they mistakenly believe is expected of "real men."

There's no need for you to be diplomatic with him. On the contrary, telling him in a delicate way not to annoy you will often have the opposite effect. Therefore, it's okay to be direct with him. At the first hint of a sexual innuendo, let him know that you consider his behavior to be childish and low-class. Give him both barrels, and refuse to listen to his denials. If he persists, pointedly ask for some identification so that you can be precise when you report his behavior to *his* superior.

Don't let yourself be convinced that "he doesn't mean any harm"; that's one of the ways he gets off the hook. Besides, he *causes* plenty of harm whether he means to or not.

There's also a personal benefit to dealing effectively with those who through their rudeness foster a climate of sexism: it impresses your boss. You'll be amazed at what making Joe understand that you're there to work and not to joke around does for your reputation and status around the company. For instance, Elizabeth only had to apply the frost to Joe one time. Not only has Joe treated her like a professional since then, but her boss told her the other day that he was gratified at how she'd "matured" since coming to work for him. It looks as if people are beginning to stop thinking of her as "that sweet young thing."

• *Francine's Story: "Come and Get It"* •

I hired Francine away from another personnel firm where she'd enjoyed the reputation of being a "good producer." Most of the accounts she could bring us seemed to be quite small, but we had some larger accounts on which I thought she might do well.

Physically, she was of normal height and build, with a pleasant face. She was what I used to call "nice looking" when I tried to fix my brother up with a blind date. You know the type: a lot like you and me.

The first couple of weeks, she familiarized herself with our operation. She came in every day dressed in a conservative blue or gray suit, never anything flashy. Her hair was always neat but not distinctive, appropriate to the modest amount of make-up she wore. When she felt comfortable with us, I sent her out to work for a week on a salary survey project we were doing for one of our clients so that the consultant working that account could have a well-earned vacation.

She reported to the client, a big commercial real estate management company, on Monday. On Tuesday, the personnel director called me and said that they wanted to put the project on hold until their regular account executive came back from her vacation.

I said, "Why not let Francine continue to do some of the work, at least make some of the competitive salary checks, in the meantime? I know she's a new face for you, and for us too, of course, but I can assure you that she's very experienced in the area of—"

"If it's all the same to you, Diane," he cut in, "we'd rather just hold off."

"Well, sure. It's only a week, after all. But this is a little peculiar. We don't have a problem, do we?"

"No, no. No problem. Not exactly."

It's been my experience that when people say "not exactly," what they mean is "exactly." I pressed him and finally he said: "Look, this is really embarrassing. But we've done business with your firm for years. Never had anything less than professional relations. But this new Francine . . . . Well, we just can't deal with the way she's coming on to all the men down here. Not at all what we expect from your company."

He went on then, though not without a great deal of urging, telling me how Francine was lowering her voice huskily when talking to the men and cozying up to them just like a cat.

"Francine?" I said.

"Francine," he said.

He told me how she was batting her eyes at the men and acting coy, like a precocious child.

"Francine?" I said.

"Francine," he said.

He told me that her clothes and her make-up were too extreme for their conservative line of business, and that the company found itself embarrassed by her appearance.

"Francine?"

"Francine."

I apologized and offered to take the responsibility as one does when an employee behaves incorrectly. He let me off the hook as an old and valued client does. (Though not without accepting a discount on the project as an earnest of good faith.) He then said he would send Francine back to my office. I said I would be waiting.

I wouldn't have believed it was the same woman. Skirt cut up to here. Blouse cut down to there. Make-up that Cindy Lauper would call heavy.

"Francine?" I said.

"I don't understand it," she said. "I always dress my best when I go to a client's office. Only they don't seem to appreciate it over there."

As we talked, it became apparent that Francine wasn't even aware of doing anything differently from what she had been. During the first weeks in our offices, she was surrounded mainly by professional-looking women, so she looked and acted like everyone else. But her appearance and her coquettish behavior were a guise that she automatically and unconsciously adopted whenever she was around men. I began to understand why she had no big clients; that kind of behavior is seldom tolerated by big firms, which are always conscious of their public images.

Francine typified today's gender confusion. Did she want to be sexy? Did she want to be professional? Could she be both at once?

Many of us women suffer from the sexual schizophrenia that results from the conflicting needs to be thought of as both provocative and professional at the same time. That's because our early programming makes us need to look attractive to men, while our contemporary programming makes us need to be professional and businesslike. So we're ambivalent about how we present ourselves, which makes some of us try to have it both ways at once.

As Francine's case shows, that really can't work. If you try to have it both ways, you send out conflicting signals. Consider how you'd feel if you noticed that your doctor had dirty fingernails. What you'd observe with your senses wouldn't square with your mental image of what a professional should be. That's the kind of conflicting signals you send out when you try to act and dress provocatively while simultaneously insisting loudly on your professionalism. It makes it difficult for people to predict your behavior. To the extent that you send out such signals, you share at least some of the responsibility for any sexual harassment that results from it.

I know the suggestion that women might own a share of the responsibility for some harassment at work will be unpopular with some women. Some women need to feel that men are always the troublemakers and that women are always their prey.

It's rare, however, that sexual harassment in the workplace is completely uninvited—not impossible, just rare. The next story tells about just such a case. But in many instances, neither party can successfully claim innocence. In fact, my attorney informs me that most successful court defenses involving sexual harassment are based on this very point: both parties contributed to the escalation of the situation.

• *Gloria's Story: The Casting Couch* •

It seems like one of those things more likely to have happened in the days when Simon Legree could hide behind his cape and twirl his mustache villainously while bending helpless women to his will. Yet Gloria, uneducated and naive, and having two children to support, found herself in the unenviable position of having to accede to her boss's desires in order to keep her job.

She came into our offices not long ago, looking so forlorn and wasted that our receptionist almost turned her out. But I'd heard her pleading that "I'll take anything, anything. Just help me get out of there." The sight of her aroused my pity as well as my curiosity, and I asked her to visit with me. She immediately told me that her boss had been demanding sex from her in order to let her keep her job operating one of the sewing machines in his small, west-side, shirt-making business.

Her case was nothing like Anna's. There were no tender emotions involved on the part of either Gloria or her boss. In fact, even passion seemed to play little part in their relationship. Gloria was rather plain, to be blunt about it, and she admitted that neither she nor her boss seemed to derive any real pleasure from each other. She said that abusing her simply seemed to make her boss feel like "a big shot." Anna's case seemed almost pleasant by comparison with Gloria's story.

Gloria's case compared poorly with Betty's, too. Betty was at least able to make decisions on her own and to take care of herself, while Gloria only seemed pathetic and helpless.

Even compared to the case of Denise and her "assistant," Gloria came off poorly. At least Denise's assistant was very well compensated financially for his trouble, whereas Gloria was paid only a little more than the minimum wage.

All things considered, cases involving a woman's forced choice between abuse and unemployment are the saddest of all. They almost always involve deliberately degrading someone. They are a form of nonviolent rape. Laws are supposed to protect workers from that kind of viciousness, but laws don't always work.

After Gloria finished pouring out her tale, I told her I was sure we could find a position for her in no time at all so that she could get out of her present situation. This was a pretty big leap of faith on my part, because none of our clients had ever asked us to help fill positions anywhere near Gloria's income level. We were accustomed to handling positions in the medium-to-upper ranges, and that's how our clients thought of us. They only contracted us for their more senior positions. But this time I wanted to make an exception to our usual standards and practices, even knowing that one hour of one of my consultants' time would cost more than any fee we could possibly derive from helping Gloria.

"Gloria, after what you've told me, I can't imagine why you've stayed there as long as you have," I said.

"It's because of my babies," she said. "I can't just walk out on my job. I've got to have income."

"But couldn't you find another job?"

"I got no skills. Can't type or anything. Can't even talk very good, to tell you the truth."

"Still, there must be *something* you can do. Why haven't you at least tried?"

She kept her eyes down. "Who would want me? Don't know how to do nothin'."

Her self-image was in terrible shape, and whose wouldn't be under the circumstances? I ripped the first chapter of a book about job hunting that I was working on out of its binder and handed it to her.

"We'll find you a job, don't you worry," I said. "But first, this manuscript explains the attitude that brings success to job applicants. And it tells you how to get that successful attitude. I want you to go back to the waiting room and read it all the way through while I make some phone calls, okay?"

She didn't put out her hand. Instead, she lowered her head a little more.

"Go ahead," I said, shaking it under her nose, "take it. Don't be bashful."

With every shake of the manuscript, her head fell a little more until it was almost between her knees. She still didn't take the papers.

What in the world was wrong with the child? I'd ripped up my manuscript for her! I felt I deserved a little more cooperation than I was getting.

I heard my voice get stern. "Will you read this as I told you?"

Suddenly a tear plopped to the floor. "Can't read, neither," she said in a small voice.

That complicated my task of finding her a job, I'll admit. But more than anything else, it made me understand the victims of forced sexual abuse on the job. They are not the connivers like Betty. They are not the tenderhearts like Anna. The Annas and the Bettys enter into their relationships willingly and more or less knowledgeably.

Gloria, on the other hand, helped me to understand that those coerced into relationships that disgust them in order to keep their jobs are the weakest, neediest, and least informed of women. It has always been so. In fact, the term for such a deal, the "casting couch," refers to the exchange of Hollywood acting jobs for sexual favors. And, true to type, the victim of the casting couch seems generally to have been the kind of woman who otherwise couldn't have gotten into the movies unless she bought a ticket.

The casting couch still exists in many industries today in spite of all the laws designed to protect workers. Those who use it have just made sure they victimize the younger, less-informed, less-secure women, who are unlikely to know what steps can be taken to secure their rights.

As things turned out, I guess Gloria's boss couldn't learn to live without force. Rather than consent to the court order my lawyer got directing him to "cease and desist" from harassing his female employees, he closed his little sweatshop down. We were able to place his three female and two male employees in better-paying jobs.

Not exactly a happy ending, but better than the beginning.

• *Helen's Story: The Diplomat* •

Helen did not get involved with her boss. But that wasn't because he didn't try. His approaches to her were serious, not just annoying like the ones Joe was always making to Elizabeth. So she didn't have the option of laughing them off.

He wasn't a lout like Gloria's boss. In fact, he was rather sophisticated and desirable. So she couldn't ignore him as just another creep.

Her job was a good one, well paying with a future. She basically liked her boss and found him good to work with in every other way. She liked the company, she liked her co-workers, and she didn't want to quit.

Yet she was in my office considering accepting another job. It was one of the few times I ever talked myself out of a fee. I told her she'd be better off learning to deal with her boss's unwelcome advances than taking a new job in order to avoid him.

She had already behaved as if she knew the first rule: discourage advances from the outset, don't give things a chance to get started. Once you're at all receptive to his advances, it makes it difficult to backtrack and call it off. Make no mistake, a man who survives his first tentative spin of the wheel will want to turn over all your letters. As Mae West said, "When women go wrong, men go right after them."

The best friend of the woman who needs to discourage an advance is diplomacy. That's the art of saying "Nice doggy!" until you can find a rock. Your way of saying "Nice doggy!" is to keep any discussion on a purely business level. For instance, be on your guard when you have lunch with a man.

Lunch is one of those occasions when rituals of romantic exploration are common. This is especially true for those in white-collar professions where lunch has strong social overtones. The prescription is to change the subject when anything that is too far away from business is mentioned. Keep the talk on business, and avoid anything personal.

That advice is for your behavior at lunch. My advice about dinner is different; try to avoid having it with him, even if you're traveling, which is not unusual for female professionals today. If you avoid seeing him for dinner, you won't have to deal with keeping his remarks on business and away from personal matters. Even more importantly, you won't have to deal with the kind of man like Helen's boss: the persistent man who won't take a hint, won't take no for an answer, and pursues you as if you were an important new account.

If he won't let you confine your discussions mainly to business and always tries to make them personal, steer the conversation toward his wife and kids; that'll slow him down. Ask about their house in the suburbs, taxes, and his commute time.

If all else fails, bring out the big gun: ask about his golf game (that's almost always a good one). In other words, try to get him to begin thinking of you as "one of the guys" rather than "one of the girls." He may bore "one of the guys" with how he took a three on the long fourteenth hole at Run-o'-the-Mill Country Club, the one with the dogleg to the right, and so on and so on. The same man who's hitting on you may talk his buddies' ears off, but he's not likely to proposition them.

The key is to turn a man down without running him down. You probably won't get fired for rejecting his one-sided interest. But losing your job is far more likely if you're hostile or belligerent. As for accepting him, of course, you're certain to lose your job—if not now, then eventually. Remember Anna?

All in all, your best bet is to turn him down with the same respect and tolerance for his feelings that you would like him to show you if your situations were reversed. I mean you should go easy on the bum—for your own safety.

• *Irene and Jan: The Other Woman* •

A young woman of my acquaintance is a CPA with one of the "Big 8" firms in New York. Irene is young, bright, assertive, and very well trained in her specialty. As far as I know, she's rated as a top performer and is respected by both her colleagues and her clients. She's also very attractive and has always comported herself in a professional manner. In fact, she generally enjoys the reputation that Caesar's wife was supposed to have of being "above suspicion."

Irene was transferred to a new and very important office of the firm. She quickly learned what was common knowledge around there: the managing partner was having an affair with his secretary, Jan. Irene avoided hearing any more about the matter, since she knew that gossiping did nothing to promote the professional image she'd need eventually to be offered a partnership.

Jan, on the other hand, conceived an instinctive and immediate dislike for Irene, whose competence she apparently saw as competition. This turned out not to be a good thing for Irene. Somehow, Jan failed to notify Irene of important meetings. Irene's requests and messages seemed always to get lost. Irene heard remarks she'd made come back from her boss in grotesquely distorted form. After a while, she regretfully concluded that Jan was out to get her and that there wasn't much she could do. The secretary seemed to have all the aces.

Irene confronted her boss and made known her suspicions. Complaining to the boss about his lover is definitely *not* a recommended way of going about the problem. In fact, Irene found her situation considerably worsened after her talk with him. She told me that she'd about decided to find a new job.

Then we put our heads together. I told Irene that Jan was as likely as any other woman to have potential that had been overlooked. I advised Irene to take the first step toward an improved relationship, not becoming a pal to waste time with or to gossip with, but becoming a coach and trainer to the other woman. In fact, I advised Irene to avoid *any* discussions of a personal nature with Jan and to keep their discussions professional at all times.

The secretary was leery at first, as you might expect. But she ultimately came around. (Remember, we women have a strong need to form attachments of all sorts in the workplace.) Irene urged Jan to get into the mainstream of the firm by learning more about accounting. The secretary had always wanted to move to the professional side of the firm but had never received any encouragement, even though she already had a college degree. Irene helped her bone up for her accounting "boards," helped her prepare her application for admission to graduate study, and even wrote a letter of recommendation to her *alma mater*. Jan began to see Irene as an ally rather than as a threat. Irene's career got back on track as a result of having a pipeline to the boss.

It turned out to be a blessing for Jan, too. By the time the managing partner tired of the relationship and dumped Jan a few months later, she was well on her way to having her own CPA credential.

I understand Irene was the first member of the professional staff to greet the boss's new secretary and offer to buy her lunch. Irene never has to learn the same lesson twice.

CHAPTER 11

Combining Success and Femininity

Recently it was my pleasure to be a guest at the swank Union League Club in Chicago for a dinner introducing a number of African businessmen to the American market. It was the kind of affair to which a lot of notable people were invited, the kind where you keep whispering to your escort, "Hey, see the tall guy in the corner? Isn't that so and so?"

Among the bejeweled women was one very attractive young woman who was with one of our more prominent local politicians. I was sure she was a model or a movie star or something like that. She had the kind of poise, of total self-confidence and self-assurance, that women in those professions often seem to have.

Even though most of my time these days is devoted to my trading business, I'm always on the lookout for women who seem to be self-reliant. They tend to do well in the personnel business, and I never miss the chance to recruit one. So I struck up a conversation with Eleanor during the reception that followed dinner.

"So, Eleanor," I said, "where do you work?"

She named one of the air freight expediting companies.

"What do you do there?" I asked, assuming from her age that she might be a secretary or receptionist.

"I drive," she said brightly.

"Drive? You mean you drive a truck?"

"Sure. It's a great job. It pays two or three times what my friends make doing office work."

"Forgive me for being so surprised," I said. "It's just that one doesn't normally think of women being truck drivers. Especially ones as pretty as you."

"Actually, the job helps me keep my looks—plenty of exercise. But the company has a weight limitation on all packages, so it's never too much for me to handle. Maybe in the old days it required a lot of upper body strength, more than most women have, in fact, but not any more."

So she made good money and enjoyed the work. But what about the *real* reason most women would be reluctant to look for that kind of job? It's a difficult topic to ask about, especially on such short acquaintance.

"But doesn't driving a truck make you feel a little, well, 'mannish?' A little less attractive as a woman?"

She gave the only possible answer as yet another handsome man came up at that moment to ask her to dance. "Haven't had any complaints yet," she said.

Eleanor is an example of the modern woman who can take any job that she chooses to take and still be confident about her own femininity. Thankfully, she's not unique. More and more of us women are realizing that our "gender identity" need not depend on what we do to earn a living. Another example is a California woman named Gwen Adair. She looks to be about thirty and is very attractive, with a feminine mass of long hair. As far as anybody knows, she is *the only woman in the world* to practice her particular trade, even though her job pays well and looks like a lot of fun. She's the first woman licensed to referee professional boxing matches.

It would be difficult for me to believe that her job has hurt her self-confidence. I would rather think that her work has probably enhanced it. After all, a 120-pound woman who steps in between two heavyweight prizefighters and says, "All right, boys, I want a good, clean fight," is likely to develop the ability to seem at ease in most situations.

• *Threatened Femininity* •

We women often feel we aren't equal to the challenge of exciting work because, unlike Eleanor and Gwen, we perceive a threat to our sense of femininity from nontraditional work. Here's how that mistaken perception comes about. There is an image inside you of what it means to be feminine. It's like one of those props they use for trick photos—the kind where you rest your chin on a headless cutout and the photo shows the body of a cowboy or a bathing beauty with your head on it.

Every time you think about yourself, you see your head on top of that feminine image stored in your mind. The image may or may not be an accurate depiction of you. It may or may not be an accurate depiction of women in general. But it *is* the programmed filter through which you always see (and *judge*) yourself as a woman. Your picture of what constitutes femininity is another result of your early programming. Of course, if it remains unspoken and hidden, it can be just as insidious and just as hard to change as are all those other images your programming has given you.

The root of the problem is that the picture of femininity many of us have learned corresponds poorly to the new reality for women who work. Thus, we find ourselves suffering today from a kind of "gender confusion." That is, for most of us the image of the feminine ideal with which we've been programmed does not include the picture of the strong, powerful woman in charge. In fact, it almost always includes just the opposite picture: the weak, passive, dependent woman.

The error that results comes about because we cherish our frilly notions about the feminine ideal, so much so that one of our greatest fears is losing our femininity. As a result of this fear, many of us women find it necessary for our peace of mind to make an uncomfortable choice between who we *can* be and who we *let ourselves* be.

In order to continue to feel confident about our femininity, then, many of us sacrifice our potential and become less than

147

we might have become. That is, some of us subconsciously hold ourselves back, fearing success because it seems to be at odds with all that we've been programmed to appreciate as feminine. And who of us wouldn't want to feel secure about her femininity? It's a perfectly normal reaction.

The irony is that no such choice between femininity and achievement is really necessary. Being successful, being an achiever, and being the boss are not conditions that are at odds with true femininity, but only with our warped and lopsided picture of weak and ineffectual femininity. You can be both securely feminine and enormously successful at the same time. You can be in charge of hundreds of subordinates and millions of dollars of budget and still not be thought of as "mannish."

The error, therefore, is grounded in the distorted *perception* many of us have been given of what it means to be an ambitious, assertive achiever. We wrongly perceive it as unfeminine. One basis for this error, of course, is the early, girlish programming that has caused us to think of femininity the way that we do. I'm sure that by this time that statement doesn't surprise you, because I've identified early programming as a culprit so many times before. This time, however, there's another culprit as well.

• *Femininity and Men* •

This time it's necessary to specifically indict *men* as being partially responsible for one of our mistaken attitudes. What leads to their culpability in this case is the male ego, which is so fragile that it makes Wedgewood seem like Tupperware by comparison.

The modern Western male is often terribly insecure. The only way he can be sure of keeping his place is to keep you in yours. Then he knows that he *always* has *someone* to look down on, even if it's *only* you. (Don't blame me if the last sentences seem offensive; it's the way many of them feel, isn't it?)

The need to accommodate a man's ego may be one of the reasons you limit yourself. You become afraid to be too good at anything, afraid that your man's ego will be bruised if he's confronted with your competence.

Then, of course, he might leave (or at least distance himself emotionally). And one of the things we've been programmed to be very, very bad at is being alone. Most of us would rather have him with all his faults than be alone. So we let ourselves be less than we can be in order to avoid causing him to doubt his unjustified feeling of automatic and inherent superiority.

I know what I'm talking about because of my firsthand experience with the male ego. My second husband was an ex-Marine; that's strike one in the male ego game. He was also a pilot (strike two). And his hero was Ernest Hemingway; strikes three, four, and five.

I was married to him when I first decided to start my own company. He wailed like a siren when I told him. He recited every reason in the book why I was wasting my time. And you know what? Most of his arguments against my attempts to find success had no factual basis. His most effective arguments (the ones that had the most effect on me, anyway) were those that were personally belittling rather than logical.

He said a lot of the same things we women so often hear when we announce an intention to try to move ahead on our own. "*You* can make a go of your own business? Don't make me laugh." "*You* can become a lawyer? Who'll take care of the kids?" "*You* want to go to night school? Over my dead body!" Those are the kinds of arguments many a woman hears from her "significant other" when she endangers his self-assigned supremacy by asserting her independence of both thought and action. There *are* supportive, secure men out there; it's just that there are more women who want to develop themselves than there are strong, enlightened men willing to see and help their women succeed.

In fairness, though, it must be noted that our men today are in a quandary of their own over gender expectations, just as we are. Especially confused are those men in white-collar businesses who work right alongside the pink-collar work force of women. Corporate affirmative action programs have required that these men be democratic and liberal in their thinking. So, outwardly, male executives have to display what I like to call the "Sesame Street Syndrome": the loud, ringing assertion that everybody is equal and everybody is the same, just as is frequently proclaimed on the TV show. It's a beautiful philosophy.

But how much do they really mean it? How deeply have they accepted this philosophy of equality? Many men of an age to be important executives today have grown to adulthood under a culture in which women were considered inferior. We've required them to make a complete about-face in their basic beliefs in a fairly short period of time. As a result of trying to obey laws that conflict with their own early programming, some of these men have come to sound like "Sesame Street" on the outside. But on the inside, they may feel less like "Sesame Street" and more like George Orwell's *Animal Farm,* the fable about the barnyard where all the animals were equal—but where the pigs were a little more equal.

• *Men's Programming* •

Let's be fair to them: men are victims of their own programming, just as we women are of ours. They can no more help wanting to feel "a little more equal" than those pigs could. But even though we understand how they got the way they are, it's past time for them to alter their programming and come to grips with the new reality.

The programming of men that makes them demand supremacy is universal. There is a sheikh, for example, with whom I have worked closely for nearly ten years now. His wife, the sheikha, and I have become closer than I would have thought possible for women of such different cultural backgrounds. Nonetheless, only recently did I tell her that one of the reasons for my divorce from Smilin' Jack, the "Terror of the Skies," was that he'd been having an affair with another woman.

Khalila stared at me for a while after this revelation. Then she looked quizzical, as if she expected more, and said "Yes?"

"That's it," I said. "He was seeing another woman. And she was a real drip, too. Joan Collins I might have understood. But a drip!"

Again she looked puzzled. "Of course she was, as you say, a 'drip.' That was the kind of woman he needed for his mind."

"His mind? I don't think it was his mind that was his number one concern."

"Oh, but of course it was," she said. "We take a different view of men here. Men have to feel they are commanders. So we let them command. But some of you Western women can command men. So then the men must find other women to command. But they fear the strong women. So what women are left to make them feel like commanders? Ones who are 'drips.'"

I love the sheikha like a sister. But in this one instance, I wasn't sure her pragmatic viewpoint could be easily adopted by a Western woman. She's a victim of her own kind of programming, one that causes her to willingly limit her prerogatives in life in order to accommodate somebody else's wishes: ". . . we *let* them command."

Don't be misled into believing that Middle Eastern women must be subservient because they have no say in the matter. While that's true, it's also true that their system is one that the women themselves accept and help to perpetuate. The Middle Eastern women know they're not helpless and inept. *But they've learned to act as if they were.* And that's the fondest wish of Western men: to get us to behave subserviently. Our fear of violating that wish is what makes us cling so tightly to our outmoded picture of soft femininity.

Understand that men are concerned purely with outward behavior rather than with internal belief. It's not important to men what we women believe about ourselves so long as we behave meekly. The truth has nothing to do with it. Whether or not a woman is as inept as her image makes her appear to be is not the point. The system is just like the Middle Eastern system in this respect: it requires us women only to *behave* as if we're inferior. That's why women so often hold themselves back from maximum effort in their careers. Obvious success would make it impossible to maintain the fiction of female inferiority.

That's where the notion of losing our femininity begins to play such an important role among us Western women. Our men have the same need to be commanders as do the Middle Eastern men. They expect us to behave as if we were their subordinates. But society has recently acknowledged that we women are free to develop as persons in our own rights. Naturally, that makes our men nervous.

Which, in turn, makes *us* nervous.

In fact, this confusion makes us so nervous that many of us simply abdicate our rights to personhood and behave as "the old man" wants us to. Behaving the way he wants you to behave almost never results in your becoming at least as successful as he is in the workplace. That level of achievement would be too threatening to his fragile ego, and you both know it.

These are not radical ideas, of course. Many women have written on the subject of how the need to appease the male ego acts as a depressant to us. It's helping us finally to recognize that success is not at odds with femininity, only with somebody else's faulty idea of femininity. It would be best if some man could explain the same things to your man, to help him change his outmoded concepts about your success. Regrettably, until that happens he'll just stay tense, because there's not much *you* can do to calm his fears when he sees you usurping his position of supremacy. As they say, *he* owns the problem. Therefore, *he* has to solve it.

And, so far at least, nobody seems interested in helping him. In fact, my biggest criticism of the feminist movement (and I have many) is that nobody is explaining to our men what's going on. Nobody is calming their fears. Nobody is soothing their egos and saying, "There, there" when they have to begin reporting to us women on the job. Nobody is helping them get used to us. Nobody is informing them that we're still women and not men in skirts, and that everything is just the same as it always was.

Except that we're equal to them. Equal in the "Sesame Street" sense, not the *Animal Farm* sense.

• *Is Business Unfeminine?* •

If there's not much we can do to get men to appreciate an ideal of femininity that stresses equality and that includes strength, at least we can be sure that *we women* avoid misunderstanding the feminine ideal. But I'm not at all sure that we've reconciled success with femininity in our own minds yet. I'm doubtful because of that remark I heard so many times while compiling the reactions of other women for this book: "A woman shouldn't act like a man." I'll bet you've heard women say it yourself.

So, how does a man act in the business world? It seems that many of us believe male business behavior to be synonymous with brutality and cruelty. Otherwise, why would we be so worried about coincidentally "acting like a man"? And if this is really the way men behave, does that mean that fascism is a necessary personality trait for getting ahead in the working world?

In truth, neither men nor women who are respected achievers in business can afford to indulge in vicious, unstable behavior. On the contrary, the higher you go in business, the more you need such traits as diplomacy, integrity, and compassion. For example, it's typical of successful managers, whether male or female, to understand that one gets a job done *through* people and that people must be treated as though they were important, which they are. That means that getting to the top levels of most corporations is more likely to happen to a well-integrated personality than to a bully.

How is it, then, that so many of us have developed the erroneous idea that business success requires a domineering, uncaring personality, and that pushing ahead vigorously in business therefore entails a risk to our femininity? It's because of the way in which we women who work have built up experience with male bosses. What happens is that we work for the worst male bosses at the worst possible time, when we're just starting out. It's what may have happened to you on your first job. Was your immediate supervisor a man? Was he arrogant? pompous? tyrannical? It's easy to see how you might have gotten the idea that such unpleasant characteristics are the reason men are in charge.

Here's what really happened to him, however. He planned to be a top-level manager. But most upper-level managers start as "first-line supervisors" in charge of some entry-level operational area in an office or plant, right where many of us women are most likely to bump up against them. The successful men, just like the successful women, move on to the next level. But the ones who are short of people skills get frozen where they are. The reality is that men who behave inhumanely toward their subordinates are those who stall out early on the career ladder. As a result, they are clustered around lower management levels, pretty close to where they started.

Most of us women, therefore, are supervised by males in our early, entry-level, start-at-the-bottom jobs, and those males, by definition, are often the ones who didn't make it. They're cranky, and they take it out on us. They're the "secretary bashers" who burn out three secretaries a year. They're compensating for their own lack of competitive success.

The point is, that's not the way *really* successful men behave. I've met lots of them. Although most are admirable, adult role models of the Lee Iacocca type, a few have impressed me as dreadful people. So, of course, the expression "The bigger they are, the nicer they are" is somewhat of an overgeneralization.

As a general principle, however, it's true that the person, male or female, who's made it to the top behaves better toward subordinates, associates, and customers than do some of the male, first-line supervisors with whom so many of us have experience. In fact, the top executives of our top corporations tend to display qualities such as compassion and concern for their employees, which some people would classify as feminine virtues. I contend, in fact, that those "feminine" virtues are *essential* for any person, regardless of sex, who plans to rise to the top. They're *in addition* to all those so-called masculine qualities of toughness and assertiveness and so on that are also necessary to business success.

I've seldom met a senior male executive at a big company who was not mentally and emotionally tough, for example. But most of them were also fair, as far as I could tell. They weren't the fascist bullies that most women seem to think of when they talk about the way men act in business. As a result of their toughness, some of the top men I've met are feared. As a result of their fairness, some of them are loved.

But whenever they possess both characteristics, they are *respected*.

Any woman who's concerned that business might tempt her to "act like a man," then, might want to reconsider. Maybe the error of letting your femininity be threatened is really committed by the woman who tries to act "macho." In other words, it's true that being aggressive and combative and pugnacious and all those other "macho" behaviors will detract from your appeal as a woman. However, if you're honest about it, you'll have to conclude that they're behaviors that detract from a man's appeal, too. They're behaviors that have no place in business in any event.

Your femininity is *not* one of the prices you have to pay for success in business. But some of the costs of success in the next chapter are just about as expensive.

CHAPTER 12

Counting the Cost

Unless you work in one of our big, old, eastern or midwestern cities, you might not know how diverse are their downtown areas. Take Chicago's Loop, for example. You'd expect to find offices and shops, restaurants and theaters, museums, galleries, libraries, and schools. You wouldn't be surprised to find any of those in the Loop, right?

But churches? Downtown? One tends to think of houses of worship being in residential areas, and almost nobody lives in our older downtown areas, so you might not expect to find religious buildings there.

There's a lovely church right under the el tracks, however, where the trains rumbling by shake the whole building regularly. There's another made of pinkish marble that's squeezed in between two skyscrapers made of similar material; they look almost like a matched set. Then there's a synagogue in the midst of a complex of buildings housing one of the world's biggest banks. And—most unusual of all, perhaps—there's a church in the middle of a high-rise office building. Offices on the lower floors, offices on the upper floors, and a church in between. With an old-fashioned church steeple way up on the skyscraper's roof. It's the kind of thing you just don't see in Palm Springs.

This church is down the block from my office, and I'm in the habit of stopping in occasionally, as are many people who work in the Loop. One of my visits was on a Christmas Eve afternoon, the one time when you can count on church being empty. Christmas Eve *night* is the busy season, just ask any clergyman. But on Christmas Eve *afternoon,* the people stay away in droves. That's how I happened to notice a young woman sitting off to the side this particular afternoon. We were the only two persons in the church.

I'm tempted to use the fact that it was Christmas Eve to embellish the tale, to try to make it poignant like a Frank Capra film or moving like an O. Henry story. But the fact is that the woman didn't seem in any way distressed. Actually, she looked more bored than anything else, like a normally busy person who's waiting for a delayed flight at the airport and doesn't have anywhere to go for the time being.

Maybe it was the way she sat there with a blank stare, kind of like a bag lady, but with a Fendi mink. Or maybe it was just because it was Christmas Eve. But when I was ready to leave, I did a thing I seldom do. I stuck my nose into somebody else's business uninvited.

I gestured to her to follow me and recognized her as soon as we stepped into the vestibule. Sandra owns a studio that designs everything from buildings to ballpoints, and she's quite well known. Although we'd never before met, I asked her to join me for coffee.

In the coffee shop, I soon understood that Sandra was a very candid, almost defiant person. She casually confirmed my suspicions that she had nowhere to go and nothing to do. In fact, in very short order she admitted that she had no family nearby and no friends, that she was completely alone in the world.

She was twice divorced, no longer spoke to either of her ex-husbands and, in fact, wasn't even sure where they were. She told me she had no close friends, just business associates and a couple of male acquaintances that she would call upon when she needed an escort. She didn't say anything more about her family, except that she had two children, but their father had custody.

I'm the kind of person who gets all snuffly on Christmas Eve and runs around tossing money in every Salvation Army kettle she can find. Naturally, that means I'm also the kind of person who couldn't handle Sandra's solitary holiday with a dry eye. While she told her story calmly and without emotion (brave little soldier!), I found myself devastated. I had to help because I couldn't bear the thought of her being so alone, so I invited her to spend Christmas Day at my place. I always have a houseful of family and friends on Christmas, and I thought it would be just the right prescription for her.

Before Sandra showed up on Christmas Day, I took pains to make sure that everyone was prepared to be extra nice to her. I had even sent my son out to one of those "last minute" stores the night before to pick up some little trinket so she would have a present. I was determined that *my* family would be *her* family and *my* friends *her* friends. As soon as she showed up, I made her promise that she would spend the following weekend with us. But as the day wore on, I had reason to regret this impulsive invitation.

Looking back, it's difficult for me now to be charitable when talking about Sandra. In between carols around the tree, she said that both her parents were alive and well and living in Florida, but that she didn't go to see them because "it's hardly worth it for just the one day, and I'd have to be back tomorrow to tend to business." During present opening, she said that she had a brother living back east, but "who can afford the time to keep up? Haven't talked to him in years." And over dinner, she dropped the biggest bombshell of all. She hadn't *lost* custody of her children; she had *requested* that her ex-husband accept custody because, as she put it, "My schedule doesn't allow time for taking care of kids."

During all these revelations, she also talked about her business, how she'd made it grow, how she devoted all her energies to it, how much it meant to her. It seemed she had enough time and energy for her business career. But not for her family. And not even for her own children.

I've always been thankful that Sandra called me the following day and canceled the weekend commitment. Seems she was "too busy" to let a purely social involvement take precedence over her business.

Whew, that was a close one.

• *The Costs of Succeeding in Business* •

Although the price Sandra elected to pay for her business success was excessive to my way of thinking, she has this in common with all of us women who work: we must pay some kind of price for business success, and it's only how big a price that's in doubt.

The common cliché describes the business world as a pyramid, which conveys the idea that there are fewer opportunities toward the top. Because space is so scarce up there, it costs more. Now, I assume that you've decided previously that you're willing to pay the cost of career success. That's not an unreasonable assumption; you wouldn't be buying a book on being equal to the challenge at work unless work was one of the priority items in your life, right? The achievement orientation of contemporary programming has convinced you that the "view from the top" is worth the cost. In fact, you don't even consider the cost, do you? You just forge ahead, knowing that success will come to you eventually and knowing that it will have been worth whatever it cost.

That's some faith you've got there.

Underestimating the cost of succeeding in the business world can be devastating for a woman who decides to pursue a career outside the home. There's no way you can escape paying that cost, either. That a cost must be paid for success in the working world is one of the few facts facing equally *all* the women who read this book. Not to mention every man who sneaks a peek.

Every career outside the home *costs*. The type of work you do doesn't change this fact. Success at office work, at factory work, at retail work, and at service work all *cost*. Nor does the level of your goals change this fact. Becoming a supervisor, a manager, a partner, or the owner all *cost*.

So tell me, exactly what *does* success cost? If you insist that the prize is worth the costs, you ought to be able to identify them.

Well, there's money, of course. Getting ahead costs money, and every step costs some more. Remember that chapter on making "The Investment" in yourself? Say you're a young woman working in the financial community. You're almost certain to need an MBA, a CPA, or one of the other advanced financial certificates to get very far along in that line of work. You'll probably have to pay for it yourself, and those credentials don't come cheap.

Of course, you don't have to be the Wiz of Wall Street to need to spend money when making "The Investment" in yourself. Down the block from my office, for example, is a school of cosmetology and hair dressing. Most of the students there are paying for their education themselves, and, just like the MBA, it doesn't come cheap.

And there are clothes. Generally, the higher you climb on that success ladder, the more you have to pay for your clothes. But even if you're not on any kind of corporate ladder at all—like the people from the cosmetology school who tend to work in very small businesses after graduation—you still have work clothing expenses. Are uniforms free? Will the cleaners clean them for nothing?

Of course, you may be the kind of woman who dreams of having her own business someday. If you're realistic, you'll have to admit that there are few, if any, legitimate businesses that require no start-up capital. Even that "shoestring" on which many businesses can be started is a hunk of money that—let's face facts—could be lost to you forever. New business ventures have been known to fail.

If, as most women are, you're an employee rather than an employer, you still need to think about all the dollar costs necessary to supporting your career. Transportation can be a big one, of course, whether you drive or take public transportation. Then there's lunch. Babysitters. Day care. And, in more and more families, adult care for parents. Sometimes, hiring people to do the odd jobs you don't have time for. It all adds up.

And up and up.

So what you really need to consider is how much *net* financial success you should expect after deducting all these monetary expenses. You may discover that the *net* benefit after all these costs is not so great as you had hoped. Now, I know that your continued hard work will bring salary increases. But remember that some of your expenses keep pace with your income, at least for a while. In the early years of almost every woman's career, in other words, she tends to find herself disappointed financially because of the high monetary costs associated with career start-up.

• *Not Just Money* •

Of course, money costs aren't the only costs. In fact, they're the least significant costs. There's also the cost to that relationship with your "significant other" that we discussed in the last chapter. No matter how much we may bemoan it, some men resent and will not accept the lifestyle of the important woman. There's that strain to his fragile ego that occurs when you begin to make more money than he does. There's the jealousy that starts when you have to stay late three nights in a row or when you have to go out of town.

In other words, you preempt the possibility of a meaningful relationship with a large segment of the male population; you limit the number of men to whom you can relate successfully. That may be one of the costs you say you're willing to pay, but what if one of these men already happens to be your husband?

That was the case with a woman who worked for my personnel company some years ago. Liz was married to an amiable but rather bland and aimless young man when she first came to work for me. I never did find out exactly what Jack did for a living, but she let me know that their financial condition was close to perilous. It was clear that Jack didn't feel driven by a need to succeed.

Liz started working for me sometime in the summer. She worked hard, learning the business, making contacts. By Thanksgiving, she knew what she was doing. But that's getting into the slowest time of the year in the personnel business; who changes jobs around Christmas? What it came to was that, although she had made more money than she would have made on her old job, she'd been working hard and putting in long hours to do it. Those were costs she was willing to pay to get started.

That winter Liz slipped on the ice and broke her leg. There were some medical complications of some sort that kept her out for months. By the time she got back, her contacts were stale, and she had to start over almost from scratch. She was just getting on a roll when the winter holiday season came around again. For the second year, she earned far below what she and I both knew her potential was.

While all this was going on, her husband stood by her like a brick. When she was depressed at her slow progress, he cheered her up. When she expressed shame at her poor showing, he told her it was okay. When she said she was determined to continue, he urged her on. The other women in the company all envied Liz for the strong support she got at home.

After the holidays, Liz went back to her hot streak. Through the spring, she began to start earning the kind of money our other consultants were getting. By summer, she was earning at a rate well into six figures and was breathing down the backs of our top people.

By Labor Day, she announced that she and Jack were filing for divorce. She claimed that he wouldn't let her spend any money. He insisted that they live on his salary, which was very modest compared to hers. She said she wanted to enjoy her money. "Oh, sure," he said, "*your* money, *your* money. That's right, throw it up to me." And so forth. You know how it goes.

The fact is, the serious pursuit of a career by *either* partner puts a strain on *both* partners in *any* marriage. But in cases like that of Liz and Jack, where the wife is more successful at work than the husband, the strain often goes to the breaking point and beyond.

There are lots of Liz and Jack cases, and as we women increase our earning power, the number of such cases is likely to grow. It's really not unusual for a man to feel betrayed when his wife becomes more successful than he is. Men don't easily accept being bested economically by women, or even *equaled*.

• *Men, Marriage, Family* •

That last fact makes men a sort of career cost. The population of men available to you are those who can deal with your independence, who are sufficiently grown up that they can enjoy your accomplishments rather than resenting them. You'll be glad to know that there are a lot of those confident men. The down side is that there are fewer of them than there are competent women who are interested in them. What you hear is true: "There aren't enough *good* ones to go around."

In other words, some women remain unmarried as one of the costs of work success. Again, that's a cost that you may be willing to bear. But make sure. *Newsweek* magazine recently published some research which concluded that women of age forty who have never been married in the past have the same chance of getting married in the future as they do of being "killed by a terrorist." That's a poor choice of words, in my opinion, which almost seems to imply that an unmarried woman might as well find a Libyan with a machine gun to put her out of her husbandless misery.

In any event, it turned out that the data (and the conclusions) needed a whole lot of qualifying; lots of letters from readers and a number of subsequent articles in other magazines were needed to straighten the mess out. Sadly, many women read only the original article (or worse, heard about it), which made them feel that a part of life had irretrievably slipped by.

What was most interesting about this episode, however, was the truly astonishing amount of mail the magazine received on the subject. Some of the letters said, in effect, "Who cares?" Others said, "I'm over thirty, and you've scared me half to death." But the specific responses of the women were less interesting to me than was the incredible *volume* of mail they generated. It showed that there was a lot of interest among women out there about marriage and a career at the same time. Regardless of the faults of that *Newsweek* article, it did point up in a forceful way that marriage is sometimes one of the costs of a career.

Other possible costs of success that are related to your marital status involve your children. What's happening is that those career women who do find satisfactory mates are sometimes deferring their families until later and later in life. It seems to be a persistent trend. According to Princeton University's Office of Population Research, only slightly more than a quarter of women between the ages of twenty and twenty-four in 1960 had never been married. But twenty-five years later, more than half had never been married. Furthermore, the age of first birth has increased more than three years during the same time. The cost here, of course, is the well-publicized set of health risks that are correlated with age of pregnancy. Those risks may represent a fearful cost for women who defer their children for the sake of their careers, a cost their children may share since it puts them at risk as well.

Some career women not only defer children, but they forego them altogether. It's another trend that, for better or worse, shows signs of being here to stay. In fact, the U.S. fertility rate has been constant for almost a decade now at the rate of 1.8 per woman. This is below the rate needed even to replace the current generation.

I respect all of us too much to wish to rescind another woman's legal rights. Still, choosing not to have a family seems to me a very high cost. On the other hand, if, like most women, you try to juggle the needs of your family with the needs of your job, both will suffer.

I suspect that trying to get the utmost from your career while trying to give the utmost to your family is a classic dilemma, a no-win situation. But of one thing I'm certain: your relationship with your family is likely to suffer to a greater or lesser degree, depending on circumstances, by your working outside the home—if for no other reason than that your family will be deprived of some of your time. There were many times, for instance, when I longed to go to one of my boys' baseball games and found myself heading off to London or Geneva or Nigeria or Kuwait instead. This kind of stress on family life accompanies most higher-level jobs and is a cost that must be acknowledged since it involves one of the fundamental concerns of life.

• *Time and Energy* •

Of course, one of the most widely understood costs of being a career woman is the amount of time you'll need to spend working at your success. Business's demand for your time is probably best demonstrated by a curious paradox about supervision of subordinates, namely, that those with too much to do are the ones who get the most done. There's even a saying among supervisors to that effect: "If you want something done, find somebody who's too busy to do it."

Chances are, you're that kind of busy, eager, energetic, ambitious performer on your job. Chances also are that your management knows about giving more work to somebody who's already got too much on her plate. That being the case, the busier you are, the more they'll find for you to do. It's a performance measure called "willingness to assume responsibility," and demonstrating it is good for your career. What it means, though, is that your time for yourself can decrease dramatically when you decide to vigorously pursue career success, because you'll devote so much time to your job.

Now, if you're a woman who has no aspirations to management or to entrepreneurship, you may not think that the time you devote to your job will be a big cost. But chances are you put in forty hours a week, which is quite a lot of your life, especially considering that so many women have to add five to ten hours a week of travel time. That doesn't even count the time spent every morning getting ready, putting on make-up and all that. Know what? Your career takes up more than half of your waking adult life, even if you're not trying very hard to get to the top!

Since that's so, you might as well try for the top, right? Pull out all the stops, go for broke and work your tail off in a fit of total career dedication, right? Ah, but then you can forget that forty hours a week for which most of us are indentured. Forty hours are nowhere near enough. If you want to get to the top, you'll need to figure as one of your costs that you'll have nearly zero personal time.

All this pursuit of success may affect your health. What you hear about executives often having high blood pressure, ulcers, and a bad back from sitting all day is true. In my case, you can add to the list the spinal meningitis I contracted in Africa, where I wouldn't have been in the first place if my ambition hadn't been pushing me so hard to sell some company a couple of airplanes.

• *How Badly Do You Want It?* •

It all comes down to how badly you want your success, doesn't it? If you want it badly enough, you'll pay all the costs: the financial, social, psychological, and physical costs. But not knowing what it's costing you is absurd and inexcusable. For example, I had to pretend to be amused at the T-shirt my banker was wearing when I bumped into her recently at the Chicago Jazz Festival. It had a picture of a middle-aged woman wringing her hands in despair and saying, "I forgot to have babies." Phyllis has never married, is a senior V. P. at about age forty-five, and is one of the more prominent financial professionals in town. So there's no question in my mind that she knew the costs of her career exactly, which meant that the shirt was, from her standpoint anyway, cleverly sarcastic.

Still, her shirt made me wonder about all those women who pay the costs of their careers by default, without making a conscious decision to do so, perhaps without even knowing about those costs. For example, some career women really do let their childbearing years pass without making the commitment to start a family. If that's an informed decision, fine. But when it's not, it means a woman may pay some career costs through thoughtlessness and poor planning.

That's really the basis for my admonition about examining how badly you want a career. I don't want to influence your decision. Whether you *decide* to stay home and raise a family, whether you *decide* to work part-time and not "maximize your career potential," whether you *decide* to take over IBM, or whether you *decide* to loaf around on the beach is nobody's business but yours. Clearly, however, the key word is *decide*. And you can't decide that the benefits of a career are worth the costs if you don't know the costs, can you?

As for the benefits of a career, pretty clearly, I get excited by seeing women accept the challenge of the business world. If it were up to me, there'd be lots more of us sharing that kind of excitement. So I suppose it's obvious that my insistence that you count up the costs is not meant to deter you from maximizing your career, if that's what you want to do. I just want you to be sure you want it badly enough.

Intelligence, education, experience—all the other invaluable characteristics that the achievement-oriented woman possesses—won't *by themselves* bring success. They are *necessary* for success, but they aren't *sufficient*. The only absolutely indispensable characteristic of success is *determination*.

• *Determination* •

Determination means you can't afford to be frightened off the first time you're called on to work a couple of fourteen-hour days in a row. Or the first time you need to put out two paychecks to buy one suit. Or the first time some man acts turned off because you're more accomplished than he is.

I've been working with a youth group recently, college people mostly, that brought home to me the reality of knowing the costs of your success and deciding to pay them. One young woman, Nancy, seemed to have everything she'd need to succeed in her later life. Still, she was insecure. She kept looking up stories in magazines about women who had succeeded in business and bringing the stories in to me at our meetings.

I confess that I became suspicious. Some young people make a show of extraordinary interest in a subject just to impress authority figures, and I thought maybe that's what Nancy had in mind. So I told her that I already knew the stories of most of the women whose profiles she was bringing me every week, so that the exercise was probably less effective on me than she might have thought it was. But she continued to bring in clippings about Rosabeth Moss Kanter and Barbara Proctor and Laura Ashley and Patricia Ziegler and on and on.

Nancy's sincerity became clear to me only when I finally figured out what she wanted from me. She was unable to define what separated the women from the girls, so to speak. She seemed as if she wanted me to define for her *one* single characteristic that these accomplished women had in common and that was guaranteed to lead to success.

I really wasn't able to help her much until I was watching a Chicago Bears football game one day. They lost a game that they'd been widely favored to win. When Coach Mike Ditka was interviewed, he patiently identified for the reporter several errors in both offensive strategy and execution that he felt contributed to the loss.

"Yeah, Mike," said the reporter, "but what *really* went wrong out there today?"

Coach Ditka reviewed a few defensive errors and, since the reporter kept looking at him expectantly, recited a couple of errors made by the kicking team as well.

"Yeah, Mike," repeated the reporter, "but what *really* went wrong out there today?"

Ditka looked him right in the eye and told the truth on his team: "I guess the other guys just wanted it more."

That's the question you have to ask yourself: do you want big success badly enough? Or does the other guy want it more? Because if he does, chances are he'll beat you out.

Be honest with yourself, and do us both a favor. If you can't add up the costs and honestly decide that getting to the top in business is worth the price, don't try to trick us both with phony dedication. It's okay for you to opt out of the business rat race; nobody has the right to make you try your hardest.

Except you, of course.

CHAPTER 13

Maximizing a (Mid-Life) Crisis

You're probably persuaded by now that I've met a lot of colorful people over the years through both my personnel and international trading activities. But the most colorful of all was a woman I interviewed some years ago who was a real clown.

No, I don't mean she was a diz or anything like that. I mean she was a *real* clown. You know, a *clown:* floppy shoes, baggy pants, a fright wig.

No, I'm not talking about your sister-in-law, either. I'm talking about a bona fide, Ringling Brothers and Barnum & Bailey *clown* who came in to apply for a job with me.

• An "Early" Mid-Life Crisis •

Jackie had responded to an "open call" for tryouts with the circus when she was about eighteen. She had no circus skills, but they liked what they saw in her personality. They offered her the opportunity to make "The Investment" in herself of going to clown school (yes, there really is such a place). And for the following ten years or so, Jackie enjoyed a rewarding circus career as "Slappy the Clown."

But it can be a wearing life: constant travel, little privacy, crazy hours. Now, at the age of about thirty, Jackie decided it was time for a change.

All my life, it seems, I've met people who've wanted to drop out of office work and run off to join the circus. (Me, too. And I suppose, in a way, that's what I did.) But Jackie was the only person I've ever met—or probably ever *will*—who wanted to drop out of the circus and run off to join an office. After a decade of being on the road continuously, trying to find somewhere to go in towns that weren't even on the map, and making up in a dressing room next to the animal pen, the idea of a permanent home and a place to go every morning must have seemed like heaven to Jackie.

Know what? Trying to place a clown who wants to be a receptionist is even tougher than trying to place a receptionist who wants to be a clown. Can you imagine what people said when they saw her resume? We finally got it done, but it was tougher than I'd expected.

Maybe what Jackie experienced should be called the "career crisis." But people refer to it as the "mid-life crisis," and that'll suit our purposes as long as we remember that the word *crisis* is more important to the meaning than the term *mid-life*. That means that the mid-life crisis can actually be experienced at almost any age, although it happens most often when one is ten or twenty years older than Jackie was. With all that in mind, it's clear that the mid-life crisis is a very common malady.

Jackie certainly wasn't at what I'd call mid-life, but she was showing one of the primary symptoms of the mid-life crisis: the desire to totally change her career.

• A "Late" Mid-Life Crisis •

For several years now, I've been conducting job seminars in association with WCFC-TV 38, the big religious telecaster in Chicago. One of the attendees at our very first seminar was a woman of about sixty who came up to the lectern afterward and asked to speak to me privately, as people will do. She was thinking about starting a business of her own and wanted my opinion. As it happened, we became good business friends and remained so until Bubbe (Yiddish for "grandmother") died recently.

Bubbe had never worked outside the home. A widow, she not only raised her own children, but her grandchildren as well. When the last one went off to prep school in the East, she found herself alone. To fill her time, she tried to get a job but was told that she was unemployable: too old, no skills—all the usual objections. She did some volunteer work but felt she'd like to make a little money for herself, too. The only thing she was really good at, she told me, was taking care of other people. So she decided to go into the professional grandmother business.

I suppose "pioneer" would be a better term than "go into," since I had never before heard of anybody doing grandmothering as a business enterprise. Bubbe was aware of the increasing number of "personal service companies," of course, those that provide cleaning, child care, and so forth. But she had in mind a much broader range of services that no one seemed to be providing on a one-stop basis, services so personal that they were almost intimate and that were therefore so expensive that only affluent young professionals could afford them.

For example, she thought there would be a market for someone to plan and prepare at-home dinner parties. Not for a hundred people as a caterer might do, but for as few as two persons. She would also keep track of important dates and then shop for birthday presents and so forth for her clients' loved ones. She would take shirts to the cleaners, do the weekly marketing, take her client's car for an oil change, bake authentic homemade goodies for special occasions, and on and on. In other words, she proposed to act as an indulgent surrogate grandmother to affluent young singles.

She told me that she knew lots of other women in her circumstances and that she thought a company was possible in which these women could be formed into a loose association of independent contractors whose job it would be to spoil well-to-do young adults rotten. She proposed to call it "Grandmothers, Incorporated." I told her I thought the idea was crazy.

Shows how much I know. Look, if I was good at picking businesses for which the time is right, I'd be a stockbroker or an investment banker. Anyway, Bubbe hit it big by reacting constructively to her own kind of mid-life crisis. In contrast to Jackie, Bubbe was having hers rather late. But the essential element of needing to do something different with her life was there.

• A Fork in the Road •

For most of the women who experience it, the mid-life crisis is triggered by confronting the reality that the job of being a mother is over. It's brought on, in other words, by looking back on what has been and can never be again.

But in another sense, it's also caused by looking forward down a life expectancy that science has made longer and longer, but for which science has neglected to supply a purpose.

The mid-life crisis is *not* the same thing as menopause, although they often happen at about the same time. In fact, the mid-life crisis happens to many men, too, and is the subject of much behavioral literature. In other words, while menopause is primarily a physical concern, experts recognize the mid-life crisis as primarily a psychological problem, a problem of the spirit in which both women and men find it painful to watch all the milestones of their lives pass by and fall behind.

Because menopause so often occurs at the same time as the mid-life crisis, however, its physical reality represents an additional burden to us women. That means we women have to live with the constant physical reminder of our mortality during this emotionally trying time. For most of us, these physical changes come at the same time as the social changes marking the adulthood of our children, when we're around the age of forty-five or fifty. All these physical, social, and life changes can sometimes combine to make a woman display her most self-destructive job behavior.

Think about people whom you've noticed behaving peculiarly in the workplace. Hasn't it often been the middle-aged woman who begins to complain about the environment that she's never complained about before; about how if it's not too hot, it's too cold; about how things "get on her nerves" that she never used to notice before?

If you're a young woman saying to yourself, "Boy! Is that ever true! Mary, over in Accounting, is just like that; she drives me crazy," try to be a little more charitable. Remember it's something that happens eventually to many of us. Maybe to you, too.

The most obvious symptom of a mid-life crisis is depression. But also, there's a sense of guilt because you have all the time on your hands now that your family needs you less, and you sense you should be doing something with it. You look inward a lot and keep asking yourself the question "What now?"

You begin to resent much of your life situation, particularly your husband. Little things he does (or neglects to do) get under your skin. It's not that your family life has recently deteriorated; it's that anything that's been wrong for the last twenty-five years you've never had enough time to really notice until now. But now, your awareness of problems increases. You begin to feel that nothing's interesting anymore, nothing's worthwhile, nothing's fun.

If you're forty-five, you know what I'm talking about. If you're twenty-five, you don't know and don't care. But you'll get yours; the mid-life crisis is the great equalizer among women since it happens to so many of us.

• *How We Try to Handle It* •

Our reactions to the crisis are predictable, because they're usually the same. Here are the three things that a woman tends to do (or at least threatens to do) at the onset of the mid-life crisis: go on a diet and start exercising; change her hair; and get a new and more rewarding career.

Two of those steps involve appearance, indicating that appearance is a high priority item with us women regardless of age. If you're anywhere at all on the green side of your own mid-life crisis, here's a piece of advice to help avoid the error of letting the mid-life crisis sneak up on you: do whatever it takes, starting right now, to keep your appearance as good as it can be. Take care of yourself. Eat right, stay trim, and work out regularly. It may not seem like it while you're doing your sit-ups, but staying fit is easier than trying to regain lost fitness.

As for the third step, a career change, that's really what I want to tell you about in this chapter. But first, before looking at what you bright, young types in your twenties ought to prepare for, there's one very special case of career concern that deserves to be treated separately from all others. Those of us who found our mothering experience to be especially fulfilling often react to the mid-life crisis by trying to repeat our mothering careers all over again. Only the second time around, we try to find fulfillment through our grandchildren.

This is a decision to be made cautiously. Sometimes parents welcome a grandmother's involvement; sometimes they do not. Any woman who chooses to go through her mothering career all over again must understand that there are some additional participants the second time around: the parents. And they will call the tune, not Grandma. Unwelcome grandmothering is the cause of a great deal of family friction. So don't count on having the joy of tending to your grandchildren to pull you through your mid-life crisis. That's hardly guaranteed to produce good results any more, I'm afraid.

Besides, you'll only have to face your mid-life crisis again when you're in your sixties and your second mothering job is over, as was the case with Bubbe. We can be happy that very few of us have the energy to repeat the mothering process a third time, so almost nobody has to face the crisis more than twice at most. But I think you get the idea. Whether you've been a homemaker all your life or you've been employed outside the home, there will come a time in your life when your work means more to you than it did before, because other aspects of your life are winding down.

Some of us find going through the crisis to be quick and easy; others find it to be long and difficult. But few of us are prepared for it even though it's a sufficiently important time in our lives—not just physically, but professionally as well—that it's foolhardy not to anticipate it.

Anticipate that it will be a positive turning in your life, even though that turning may be preceded by some turmoil. After all, there's no victory without a battle. The fact is that when the smoke clears away, there will be more good to be gotten out of your mid-life crisis than bad.

• *A Threat and an Opportunity* •

Why should it be called a crisis, then? Well, the truth is that every crisis has at least two outcomes, a good one and a bad one. I learned to understand this from that trip to China that I told you about earlier. One of the small, newly formed, local companies with which I was working closely used a distinctive character of the Chinese language as its logo. It was on their letterhead. It was on their business cards. It was on the door over the entrance to the industrial commune factory. It was everywhere, and one couldn't help but eventually memorize what it looked like.

My guide told me that the company's Chinese name could be translated as "Crisis," and that the particular character I'd been seeing everywhere was the Chinese character for that word. Most American entrepreneurs would shy away from calling their company The Crisis Company; it's not the kind of name designed to inspire confidence in management. The Chinese, on the other hand, not only permitted this name for their new company, but they even seemed inspired by it.

My guide explained that the Chinese character for *crisis* is made up of two other characters placed one on top of the other. One of these is the character for the word *threat*, which is how we Westerners usually think of a crisis. But the other character is for the word *opportunity*. This interpretation of a crisis as a fork in the road of life helps the Oriental mind to recognize a crisis not as a disaster, but as a turning point that can lead to a good outcome as easily as a bad one.

The importance of this for a woman is that the mid-life crisis can result in the second half of her life's being at least as good as the first. That's what Bubbe was able to accomplish. She resolved her crisis constructively by using business as the opportunity to make something new of herself. She made her later years exciting, productive, and profitable. In fact, she had a ball.

It's remarkable, though, how many of us in our twenties and thirties never think ahead to our forties and fifties. I suppose we're reluctant to look squarely at our own advancing age and mortality, just as Jonathan Swift said: "We all want to live long, but no one of us would be old."

The problem with avoiding the anticipation of our middle years is that it allows us to choose in the panic of the moment the path labeled "threat" rather than the one labeled "opportunity."

But remember all those things in the last chapter that work against your success, all those "costs" associated with a career? It's remarkable how many of them go away by the time our children are grown. For example, the financial pressures associated with early adulthood are lessened for many of us by the time we're in our fifties. Then there's release from the obligations imposed by the nature of family life itself: the time and attention needed to deal with your children and your home.

In other words, the "empty nest" can bring freedom rather than loneliness. Opportunities rather than threat. More time rather than more chores.

• *Making It Work for You* •

All these positives argue in favor of looking ahead from the mid-life crisis rather than looking back, don't they? You know what makes people seem old? Looking backward. Reminiscing about some gone good old days is a betrayal of advancing age. As the poet Edward Young said, "Like our shadows, our wishes lengthen as our sun declines," which is another way of saying what that other poet, Groucho Marx, said: "Nostalgia ain't what it used to be." Looking ahead is a more youthful and a more attractive trait in a woman than is looking back.

176

So what will you have to look ahead to? Consider a typical woman of today who has worked all her adult life and has never stayed home full-time to raise her family. She's at the age when her employer is most interested in her as a management candidate. (What? Somebody wants a woman over forty for management? Yes. Statistically, that's the best age for women to be most valued by employers. Studies by my personnel company have shown that women over forty who have been with the same company more than five years are seen by management as more experienced, settled, and seasoned in judgment than any other demographic category.) Promotion is an increased likelihood for many women after the mid-life crisis.

Suppose, however, that you've had one of those jobs where you wouldn't take a promotion if they begged you. You can't stand the place; you've only kept their crummy job because you needed the money. But after your family obligations end, your pay, while very nice to have, may no longer mean the difference between making it and not. So you'll have the perfect opportunity to go for the job you've always wanted to try but were afraid to take the risk. Or write that novel that you know is in you but you've never had the time for. Or start up that business of your own that you've always wanted (maybe even international trade; who knows?).

In other words, mid-life can be your chance to take those career risks that your circumstances made you too prudent to take previously.

It may mean the opportunity to "upgrade" yourself. If you've worked as a paralegal, how about going back to school to become a lawyer, which you could never do before because the kids kept you so busy? Or, if you've always been a secretary, how about going for your MBA, now that you've got all this time on your hands? If you work in a plant, how about studying engineering? (Only 2.3 percent of all engineering graduates in 1985 were women. Talk about opportunity for visibility!)

I think you get the idea. There is more freedom available to you after successful exit from your mid-life crisis than at any time since you were a carefree youngster. Just as Bubbe did,

177

you can make the second part of your life exciting, and there's nothing anymore to stop you.

Except for the one thing that is always out to get you and that we'll talk about in the next chapter.

CHAPTER 14

Recognizing "The Plot"

Over lunch one day, I mentioned to a male friend that I planned to include a chapter in this book on "The Plot Against Women."

"Remind me never to take you to a football game," he said.

"What's *that* supposed to mean?" I asked. "I like football."

"Yeah, but you'd never be able to make it through a whole game. Every time the players went into a huddle, you'd think they were talking about you."

He was trying to tell me that I was paranoid, seeing conspiracies where there were none. I tried to explain carefully that I don't really believe that the plot against us women is organized or formal. I don't really believe that its members carry special ID cards or have secret handshakes.

But I do believe that the plot exists in the form of attitudes and habits that permeate our society. And, if I'm to be completely honest with you, I also believe that there are a very few confirmed bigots who consciously want to see us women disenfranchised as independent adults. Of course, the reason men discriminate against women exactly as they would if the plot *were* deliberate is because the atmosphere of false ideas about women encourages it.

I tried very hard to explain all this, to make him see that I wasn't paranoid and that the world really is different for women in business than it is for men. But I don't think he believed me.

I wonder if the fact that he was entertaining me at a club where only men could be members had anything to do with that.

• *Evil and Treacherous* •

I didn't want *you* to misunderstand, so I decided to start by looking up the word *plot* in my trusty *Webster's*. It said that a plot was "a plan secretly devised to accomplish an evil or treacherous end."

The plot against women is certainly secret; it has been kept secret ever since the legislation that provides for our equality of opportunity. In fact, powerful men in business rarely discuss their true feelings toward the plot anymore, for to do so is to invite legal action if overheard.

As for the ends contemplated by the plot, they certainly qualify as "evil" and "treacherous": keeping women "in their place," dependent on men for the very means of survival; preserving an artificial distinction of labor so that the archaic notion of "women's work" is revived; maintaining an artificial pay differential so that even work of comparable worth is compensated lower for women than for men; and reinstating a social order that provided for captive domestic labor.

The part of the definition that made it a little different from the idea I wanted to convey was the word *plan*. Men have no overt, formal plan to keep us down. They don't need a plan, because their instincts are adequate to the task.

• *Sinister and Mysterious* •

The flavor of the kind of plot I have in mind is the same as that of the priest's parable in Franz Kafka's enigmatic novel, *The Trial*. Paraphrasing the parable, it's the story of a simple man from the country who comes to the big city seeking justice for some wrong that is never identified. The man goes to the court and begs admittance from the doorkeeper, who refuses him, although the door stands open before him. The man asks whether it is worth his while to wait. "Could be," says the doorkeeper.

The man sits on a stool that has been placed close to the open door. Every so often he asks for admittance and is always told, "Not yet," even though the door remains open. Knowing no other door to justice, he sits there for what eventually becomes years. He tries everything he can think of, including bribing the doorkeeper, who accepts his bribe but tells him, "I take this only so you will understand that you have done everything you possibly could. But you still cannot enter."

Finally, the man's life is drawing to a close. He asks entry one last time and one last time is refused. With his dying breath, he gasps, "Everyone strives to attain Justice. How does it happen, then, that in all these years no one has come to this door seeking admittance but me?"

"Because," answers the doorkeeper, "no one but you could possibly have gained admittance through this door. This door was built especially for you. And now . . ."

The doorkeeper smiled.

". . . I'm going to close it."

That's the flavor of the plot against women. Nothing about it is overt and obvious. Nothing about it even makes sense. But there it is nonetheless. We can look through the open door of success, but they won't let us in. We spend our lives being asked to believe that full equality of opportunity is just around the corner, that it's inevitable, that it will come soon. But "not yet."

If you're thinking, "Wow! That's really paranoid," you're tuning in to the way an ambitious woman feels in a man's world. Every sensitive woman has felt it. Failure to recognize that there is a plot against women can be a fatal error for a woman who works.

Of course, there's no evil cabal of men that sits around thinking up ways to keep us women in our place. That's not necessary to the effective working of the plot against us. All that's needed is this subtle, pervasive atmosphere that results from programming saying men are strong, competent, and responsible while women are weak, emotional, and dependent.

Most people, women as well as men, are unaware of how deeply the prejudices about women's inferiority have been programmed into us. So those prejudices can bend our attitudes toward women as surely as any deliberate and careful plan could. There's no need, therefore, for the plot to be organized and overt. One of the benefits of its covert nature, in fact, is that women can be enlisted as unknowing participants. Clearly, if the plot against women were overt, we women would not contribute to it, for to do so would mean deliberately working against our own interests, and that wouldn't make sense.

Because the plot is subconscious and instinctive, however, we women can actively participate without being aware that we're helping someone else's cause at the expense of our own. We can even be ringleaders; that is, we women are often our own worst enemies.

It takes a conscious, thoughtful effort to determine just how much anti-woman bias is in you. Or it takes an emotional shock that suddenly brings you face to face with your own hidden prejudices against other women, which is the way I found out just how biased I was.

• I Was in on the Plot •

I was flying from Chicago to Madison, Wisconsin, at the time to address a group of students. I had a light, single-engine plane that had started life as a weekend joyrider but which I had converted by adding a lot of the electronic gizmos known as "avionics." I had only recently gotten my instrument certification in this very plane. That meant I was supposed to be able to fly without looking out the window.

I say "supposed to" because of a funny thing about flying on instruments: your intellect knows how to do it long before your emotions let you. That is, you're trained to such a degree that you know all there is to know about flying without visual references, but you're scared to do it. It takes a lot of experience to overcome that kind of anxiety, and I didn't yet have enough of it.

Most urban areas are tough for private pilots to handle, and Chicago is doubly so. We have all the usual urban obstacles: lots of airports (including the world's busiest), a couple of military fields with jet fighters zipping in and out, and blobs of "Restricted Airspace" all over the charts. But in addition, we have that famous Chicago-area weather that can best be described as schizophrenic. On the day I learned about my own anti-woman bias, I took off on a Dr. Jekyll morning of calm winds and isolated, fleecy clouds. A sudden, unpredicted squall line turned it into a Mr. Hyde of an afternoon.

If you can imagine a 50,000-foot-high, furry wall being pushed toward you at breakneck speed, you have an idea what this squall line looked like. It ran from straight ahead around my left side in a wide curve. I was so fascinated by the sight of it that it actually took me a few minutes to reach the decision to turn back. I just kept staring out the left-hand window, the storm growing even as I watched it.

At last I decided that the students' education would not be imperiled if they didn't hear me speak that day, and I made a 180-degree turn to the east. It wasn't until I came out of the turn that I was able to see the cloud wall curving back to the south. The storm was actually shaped like a horseshoe.

And I was the stake in the horseshoe pit.

I decided to add all the throttle I could to try to beat the weather back home. Bad choice. About twenty miles out, it turned into a three-ring circus. If Disneyland could come up with a ride like that, their stock would go up fifty points. My stomach and I parted company several times. But there was no cause for any immediate alarm; I knew what loads the airframe could take, so I knew how unlikely it was that it would break up. The really scary part was still ahead of me: landing in fierce weather. On instruments, yet.

The only light outside my window came from the almost continuous lightning flashes surrounding the plane. Not that it made much difference: the weather was so heavy that I couldn't have seen my propeller anyway. Corny one-liners kept going round and round in my head: "There's no such thing as a 'landing'—only a 'controlled crash.'" "A good landing is any one I can walk away from." "If God had meant for me to fly, He'd have given me wings." Stuff like that.

The field said conditions were "zero-zero"—no visibility at all overhead, and none at all horizontally. In addition, there were crosswinds gusting to fifty miles an hour across the only runway. Crosswinds are the ones that try to flip you over when you get close to the ground, and they can ruin your whole day if you don't watch out. But I was running low on gas and couldn't any longer choose another field. For better or worse, I was going in.

The controller's voice giving me headings and weather advisories had been droning comfortingly in my earphones. Abruptly, the voice changed. I had been "handed off" to the final approach controller. The instant I heard the new voice, I suddenly went from being merely scared to being incapacitatingly terrified. In that moment, I forgot everything I knew about instrument flying. I forgot how to read the instruments. I lost track of my heading and my altitude. I pulled up so sharply I nearly stalled out. I was in a panic.

To this day, I don't remember the seconds that passed until I got myself under control again. I was stunned at my own inexplicable behavior, unable to identify what had triggered this episode. My situation had been precarious but stable. Nothing had changed immediately before my panic that should have caused such a crazy reaction. I was wiping the sweat off my face so I could see when an explanation occurred to me. I realized that the only thing that had changed was the controller's voice.

The new voice was female.

When I heard her voice, I must have subconsciously concluded that I was history. How could it be otherwise? She was a woman, and, according to my previously hidden bias, women couldn't handle responsible jobs like air traffic control.

I suppose she'd continued to try to raise me all during my panic attack. The first thing I heard after I got myself together was her repeating my call sign in her flat, even monotone. I yelled into the microphone, "Give me a man! Give me a man!"

There was a slight pause, and then a male voice came on. I instantly had a rush of confidence. I took a few deep breaths. In only a few seconds, I began to feel I might live after all.

Funny thing happened, though. As the new controller gave me my approach instructions, I began to notice that his voice didn't have that laconic, almost bored drawl that all the expert controllers seem to have. Also, he paused a lot, as if he was relaying instructions given to him by someone else.

Hey! Wait a minute! I thought. Maybe I wasn't as well off as I'd thought a minute earlier.

"How much experience do you have?" I demanded.

"Well, uh, I'm . . . I'm in training," he responded. "But I'm the only man on duty here at this time, so—"

A trainee! In a storm! With a green pilot!

I yelled into the mike, "Give me the woman! Give me the woman!"

She came on instantly, calm and professional. She talked me down competently and safely. I never learned her name, but she will always have my gratitude.

What she will *not* have is my apologies, and here's why. After I got to the taxiway and started to catch my breath again, I challenged her: "Why did you give me a trainee in a situation like that?"

"I thought keeping you calm would be more important than anything else," she said. "After all, it was a really tough landing . . . *for a woman.*"

Here we were handling competently together an enormously difficult situation, and neither of us trusted the other. But had you asked us, I'm sure we would both have disclaimed any bias against women. In fact, we probably would have told you about how important we both had made ourselves in professions that used to be "man's work." But the fact is that both of us suffered from a hidden bias against other women.

• *The Plot Uses Us* •

Unfortunately, that's not unusual. Some of the strongest bias against women comes from other women who resent (and

fear) their success. In fact, the hidden bias that's been programmed into each of us makes us women our own worst enemies.

The least attractive recruiting assignment my personnel recruiters handle, in fact, is that of recruiting a secretary for a
female executive. Many women find it enormously difficult
and embarrassing to report to a female boss. One of the trick-
iest assignments we ever had involved exactly that situation.

A very large insurance company in Chicago named a new
head of its legal department (which would be one of the largest
law firms in town if it weren't part of the insurance company).
This was a really b–i–g job, the kind that rates a profile of the
new incumbent in *The Wall Street Journal*. As it happened, the
new department head was a woman.

The day her appointment was announced by the board of
directors, the secretary who had helped the retiring department head for years quit rather than report to a woman. It was
intended to be some kind of a grand gesture, I suppose, but it
only served to identify the woman who quit as a dupe in the
plot. So, the company dutifully posted the job opening and sat
back to wait for applicants from inside the company. After
about a month of sending her work to the typing pool and
hiring temps on a daily basis, the new chief called on me.

Normally completely self-possessed, her wheels came off in
my office. She ranted for ten minutes about women being their
own worst enemies. She understood the plot very well. After a
while, I told her there was no alternative but to offer extra
incentive pay and chalk it up as a cost of doing business.

Even with extra pay, it could have been a tough hire. But I
knew the recruiting business pretty well. I knew that only
somebody who had been the victim of a plot could see past her
prejudice to appreciate what a fine opportunity this was. I
called a woman I'd met through one of my consultants only a
few weeks earlier. Her skills were outstanding, she had about
half a law degree from night courses, and she had a wonderful
personality. She was working for a temporary agency because
she was finding it difficult to secure permanent employment.
Prospective employers always found some logical reason why
she wouldn't do, but she always understood that it was because she's a midget. I put the two of them together and earned

a fat (and easy) fee, plus getting a very satisfied client in the bargain.

It's crucial for more of us women to try to deal with our prejudice so we can learn to tolerate each other in the working world. If we don't, the plotters will win out. We will continue to be treated as if we didn't matter as much as men in the business world.

Here's a good example of that treatment. There's a type of insurance that companies take out on the lives of top executives. Should the executive die during the term of the policy, it compensates the company for the loss of service that presumably results until someone else can take over the job. It's called "key man" insurance. Key man insurance is usually required by an entrepreneurial company's bank to secure credit. Debbi Fields, the founder of Mrs. Fields Cookies, tells the story of how her bank requires key man insurance on the life of her husband, Randy, who is one of the people essential to the company.

But they have not required it on *her* life.

Her bank may be in on the plot. Her bank may suffer from the pervasive programming that says women are not important in business. It's a very common conclusion. Every businesswoman has had the experience of having someone assume, quite loudly and openly, that there's a man behind the scenes pulling her strings. Barbara Porter is head of an important firm named Porter and Goldberg. (Actually, she's *both* Porter *and* Goldberg, but most people don't know that.) When she calls on a potential new customer, she often hears the assumption that *Mr.* Goldberg is back watching the office. She jokes that she could have 100 percent of the profits but only 50 percent of the headaches because she could blame Goldberg for anything that went wrong if she wanted to. I'll bet she could get away with it, too, because most people would never doubt that there was a man behind all the business success of a woman.

• *The Real Victims* •

I'm not upset at the plot against women just because it makes our success a little tougher to come by. After all, we need challenges to enrich life. The obstacles placed in our way make us better whenever we overcome them, just as Nietzsche said: "That which does not kill me makes me stronger."

And I'm not upset just because a woman has to work twice as hard as a man to get the same recognition.

And I'm not upset that the word heard most often in response to our plans and goals is no. Actually, I consider no to be a vitamin; whenever I run afoul of the plot, I grit my teeth and remind myself silently that "Vitamin No helps me grow." I know it might sound like a corny expression, but it beats letting them get to me.

No, none of that really upsets me. Much, anyway. What really upsets me is a lot of social research done over many years that demonstrates beyond any reasonable doubt that people behave pretty much the way you expect them to. In the case of women, if the world expects us to be inept and scatterbrained, that's how many of us will turn out to behave.

People tend to live down to our expectations of them, in other words. That's why almost any woman who becomes successful in business gains a reputation as a maverick. No matter how skillful she is, no matter how professional her behavior, no matter how intelligent or accomplished she may be, a successful businesswoman is automatically thought to be a maverick.

So what does this imply for other women who have not yet maximized success in their working lives? If the world expects them to be inept and useless, and if the world thinks women who are not inept and useless are freaks, how is your daughter likely to behave?

She's likely to live down to the world's expectations of her. She's likely to amount to less than she could—often far less. As Cervantes said, "Every man is as Heaven made him, and sometimes a great deal worse."

You can't change the world's opinion of women all by yourself. But you can change your expectations for your daughter. If you act as if you expect excellence of her, you still *might* be disappointed, but if you don't, you *surely* will be.

That's what concerns me so about the plot. It doesn't threaten me personally anymore. I've got mine. So have all the other businesswomen I keep mentioning. But the younger you are, the more the plot is a personal threat to you. Ignoring the existence and the reality of the plot is playing right into their hands, a mistake that will produce another passive, submissive underling.

Don't let them have their way. Begin to fight back by fighting your own bias against other women, by showing that you trust other women in the role of superior as well as peer. Patronize the businesses owned by other women. Believe that we women have a lot going for us that can make us into good businesspeople as well as good wives and mothers.

CHAPTER 15

Appreciating Yourself

I started this book by telling you that we women have habits that cause us to commit the same errors in our working lives time after time, and I told you that they were the mistakes we women make simply because we've been brought up to be women. It almost sounded as if inferiority in the working world were our destiny.

The sentence that ended the last chapter, however, urged you to believe that we have a lot going for us that can make us into good businesspeople as well as good wives and mothers. That's far more hopeful. It almost sounds as if *achievement* in the working world is our destiny.

There's nothing inconsistent about those two statements. What has happened over the last generation or so is that the self-image of many a woman has been shaped by everybody but herself. By her early programmers: her parents, her relatives, her teachers. By contemporary programmers: success books, women's magazines, movies. By men who may have been brutal, abusive bosses, who may be nonsupportive and jealous boyfriends or husbands, or who may just be victims of their own early programming. By other women who are suspicious and envious of her determination to be an achiever and who belittle her efforts to grow.

When we begin to believe about ourselves what all those programmers tell us, they've done a good job. Rather than feeling confident that our God-given talents are adequate for success in the working world, we women limit ourselves willingly to preserve the soft self-image we've been taught is the only way to be.

• *Our Virtues and Talents* •

We need to reduce the conflict between who we can be and who we've been programmed to believe we *must* be. So many a woman lets her talent be corrupted. She lets her natural caution be turned into cowardice instead of prudence. She lets her natural need to share become dependency rather than cooperation. She lets every natural virtue become a wimpish parody of itself. Then, of course, she goes around acting in self-defeating ways and wondering why she can't get ahead on the job.

But what would happen if she stopped letting her abilities be distorted by all those programmers? What if her natural need to be with others was elevated to a capacity for understanding other points of view? Wouldn't that help her be a good negotiator and manager? What if her natural need for nurturing was elevated to a sense of closeness to customers? Wouldn't that help make her a good salesperson?

Any natural tendency can be developed to either of two extremes. The tendency to want to help others can be turned into dedication or into subservience. The tendency to appreciate order can be turned into a sense of organization or into fussiness. In the case of women, many of our natural virtues have been turned into the behaviors that fit the image of "woman" that's been programmed for us. These are sometimes the opposite of the behaviors that fit the image of "achiever" in the working world.

We are as likely as men, however, to have all the basic talents of achievers. In fact, are not many of the characteristics that we've talked about the very same characteristics that are needed for success in business? All we need is to learn to see ourselves differently. We need to learn that competence and independence are qualities that don't interfere with our estimates of ourselves as women.

191

• *The Golden Age* •

It's important to make that adjustment now. I really do believe that we're on the verge of a major shift in the working world, and you want to be able to cash in on it. We are changing from a society of "makers," which puts a premium on physical strength and stamina, to a society of "doers," which puts a premium on cognitive ability. Therefore, certain kinds of work, specifically white-collar work where we are at no physical disadvantage, will be increasingly valuable to society. We can enter into this "service economy" easily, in some cases more easily than men, and we are protected by law from unreasonable barriers to our advancement.

The day is coming soon, in other words, when being the president of the bank, the manager of the skyscraper, the senior partner of the ad agency, the owner of the real estate firm, the vice president of the conglomerate, and the director of the brokerage house will no longer be considered "man's work" or "woman's work" but "winner's work." Important work will be the province of the talented and the competent, without regard to gender.

So start adjusting your attitude now. Begin to see that you can be strong and still be a success at being a woman. That you can be independent and vital and important and busy. That you can be in charge of your own life and of all those who will report to you and respect you, not because you're a woman or because you're a brutal boss, but because you're *good*.

The confusion that we've experienced in this generation and the prejudice we've experienced in the working world have really only been strengthening processes. And they've worked. They've gotten us ready to assume our rightful (i.e., equal) place in the business world.

That must surprise those who have worked so hard to keep us down. But they shouldn't be surprised. It's just as Nancy Reagan once said, "A woman is like a tea bag: you never know just how strong she is until she's been in hot water."